My Life with a Borderline:
My Personal Journey

Matthew Kelleher

Dedicated to
Liam, for showing me the escape-hatch, and to
Shari Schreiber for helping me believe there was
life at the other side...

Prologue

I am not a psychiatrist, nor a psychologist. I have no 'training' in mental health issues whatsoever. I want to make that clear from the outset. What I am, is a 'simple' layperson who has been trying to 'make sense' of a particularly harrowing two-year period in my life. And this book is written from that perspective.

Personally, I don't like 'labels'. But we all use them, and live with them; they help us understand complex concepts and relationships that if unlabelled, remain just a jumble of ephemeral observations.

This book is written about my relationship with someone called Yvette, whom I had a two-year relationship with. Obviously, Yvette isn't her real name, and other names and places in the book have been changed to maintain anonymity.

Whether or not she did indeed have 'Borderline Personality Disorder' is irrelevant. During our relationship Yvette was never diagnosed with a condition with that name, although I do believe she exhibited the vast majority of the personal characteristics associated with that affliction.

In the same vein, whether or not I am psychologically defined as 'Co-dependent' is not relevant. Let's just say instead that her characteristics of a chronic fear of real or perceived abandonment, coupled with her emotional dysregulation and extreme impulsivity were mated and enmeshed with my own fears of abandonment and lack of self-worth.

As I said, I don't like 'labels'.

What _is_ relevant is that this book hopefully tells the story of a particularly dysfunctional relationship, and my 'journey' through that. Unlike other books about relationships with 'Borderline' people, I have tried to focus on myself throughout the book. After all, the old cliché: 'It takes two-to-tango,' continues to have resonance, probably more so in the 'dysfunctional dance' associated with a Borderline relationship.

Whilst reflecting on my relationship in writing this book, I discovered things about myself that had remained undiscovered for many years. And that is the hope I want to share; that is why I hope you are reading this.

Yes, the day-to-day dynamics of any relationship are important; 'what' and 'where' is all part of telling a story. But much more important is the 'why'. Epistemology, or 'knowledge' is at the root of Western Philosophy, and this book can hopefully be regarded as an epistemological 'journey' into discovery about oneself.

'Borderline Personality Disorder' can be a very destructive condition. But so can the character traits of those people who 'choose' to have relationships with 'Borderlines'. And at the end of the day, although I suffered immense pain during my relationship with Yvette, I only had myself to 'blame' for remaining in a position of harm for as long as I did.

However, I'm beyond 'blaming' myself for that now, as the experience has reawakened things about myself, and indeed my 'Self', that I had been unaware of for the whole of my life to date.

Writing this book has been catharsis for me; it has allowed me to realise positive change within myself, by providing me with the opportunity to reflect on my experiences in the recent past, and committing them 'to print'. And I truly hope that if this book 'speaks' to you, then reading it can help you to move towards a greater understanding of yourself.

If you're reading this book to find out about the specific psychological characteristics of 'Borderline Personality Disorder', then I'm afraid you're reading the wrong book. If this is what you are looking for, then I would suggest you consult respected, learned academic guides out there, of which there are many.

But if you're currently in, or have just left a relationship with someone whom you suspect has 'Borderline' characteristics, then you're in the right place. This is not a book which (unfairly) 'persecutes' people with these particular characteristics.

It is a story about *self*-analysis and *self*-discovery, and that should be your only reason to read ahead.

One of my hero's Thomas Szasz couldn't have expressed this any better when he said:

'People often say that this or that person has not yet found himself. But the self is not something one finds, it is something one creates.'

So good-luck in creating *yourself.* Enjoy the journey of discovery, and look within yourself, because you only have your *'Self'* to be responsible for.

Matthew Kelleher
January 2012

Chapter 1

My soul was filled with despair and an overwhelming sense of loss.

'Why didn't she want me? Why didn't she love me? All I ever wanted to do was to love *her*.'

I had been un-ceremonially 'dumped' by text a few days earlier. And my head was spinning with questions: 'Why? What was *wrong* with me?'

My feelings of inadequacy and self-loathing reached a crescendo as I logged onto my PC in my study. I *would* find someone who would love me, someone that I could love, and live my life for. I logged onto 'findyourmatch.com' and reactivated my personal profile *yet* again.

What doesn't kill you makes you stronger, right?

Little did I know what was about to happen.

It was Thursday night, and I'd already had a couple of glasses of wine too many. In my semi-drunken stupor, I searched the profiles of single women in the local area. Page after page of profiles danced before my eyes.

'Boring housewives with two-point-two children,' I thought, as my despair returned.

Surely there was someone out there who could make me feel alive and take away this pain? It was getting late, and I had an early start the next morning. Midnight approached, and I promised myself to retreat to bed before the next day arrived. In one last attempt, I extended the search radius.

'Thirty-miles - that would be it'; I promised myself bed after this.

I clicked on the 'Search' button and waited indifferently for the results. I only wanted to see profiles of people who were 'Online' at that moment, in search of an immediate connection to allay my depths of despair. I needed someone, *anyone*. And I needed them now. I flicked through the first couple of profile pages, and was a few seconds away from ending my futile search.

And that's when I saw her, the person that would, unbeknown to me at that time, change my life forever…

My semi-conscious, alcohol-induced coma was cured as I eagerly scanned her profile. Her profile pictures painted an image of joy and beauty; an illusion, a 'mask' that I was later to find out concealed something much more dangerous.

In her profile she talked of her passion and her love for life; that she cared, and gave herself to others almost 'unconditionally'. She talked about love and loss in a vulnerable, almost child-like narrative:

'It is better to have loved and lost, then never to have loved at all.'

This was an inextricable connection between love and pain that I would all too soon learn to endure all over again.

My heart raced as I quickly composed an email.

'Please don't go offline!' I thought, as the message 'Email sent' flashed upon the screen.

I sat there, waiting; anticipating a message in return.

'Had I been too keen? Had I been to open?' Doubts flooded my mind as I sat there, transfixed to the screen, waiting, waiting…

Then it happened. I had a new email. I feverishly clicked on my inbox. It was her! She'd replied! My mood shifted from depression to excitement.

I quickly returned her communiqué with questions, so many questions… 'What did she do? Where did she live?' I wanted to know *everything*, and I wanted to know it *now*.

Her name was Yvette, and she was a doctor. But how? How could I have been so lucky to find this beautiful Rose within a meadow of 'Daisies'?

Midnight came and went, as I renegaded on my promise to myself. The drive next morning would mean an early start, but my mind was taken over with thoughts of this elusive, enchanting creature. Without even speaking to her, she made me feel 'alive' like no-one I had ever 'met' before. Before I knew it, we had exchanged mobile telephone numbers and I was at last released from my PC to retire to my bed.

But it wasn't sleep I was after; it was her.

Texts were exchanged, fast and furiously, well into the early-hours of that Friday morning. I couldn't compose them fast enough on my archaic mobile, totally inept compared to her new smart-phone. Before I knew it, I was telling her my deepest, darkest secrets.

Honesty is a respectable virtue, isn't it? I thought.

'I hope U don't think bad of me, but I had an affair,' I texted, anticipating but simultaneously dreading that this may be the last I hear from her.

To my delight, she admitted the same, and that's when I knew; I knew that I could be *completely* honest with her. I had confessed my greatest 'sin' to her and she *still* wanted me.

I gave more and more of 'myself' to her; little did I know that everything I was giving of myself so freely that morning would later be used to persecute and torture me in the months that would follow.

3

I fell asleep, a deep slumber filled with dreams of love and passion that turned out to be delusions in the nightmare that was about to unravel...

My alarm-clock aroused me at five. I had a long drive ahead. But my thoughts weren't on the presentation I was giving later that morning; they were with *her*.

'When are we going 2 meet? X' I eagerly texted.

After texting back and forth, we set a date for Sunday evening. Only forty-eight hours to wait. And they couldn't pass quickly enough. She told me she was out with friends that Friday night, and that she had a date with someone else on the Saturday night, which had been arranged for a while.

On Friday night I sensed alcohol in her bloodstream as she incessantly texted me from the toilets of the club she was at; messages depicting how a group of men were chasing her, wanting to literally devour her. I felt a pang of jealously.

'But surely she was *mine*?' I thought. 'I had told her *everything* last night?'

She revelled in her narcissism, and I struggled with myself to maintain a grip on my emotions. I hadn't met her yet. So why should I feel jealous?

She got home late, at about two on Saturday morning. A message flashed-up on the screen of my mobile, disturbing my slumber:

'Why RU still on findyourmatch?' she enquired.

I was confused. I hadn't used my PC since Thursday night. But why did I want to suspend my profile anyway? I hadn't met Yvette yet, and I didn't feel the 'need' to suspend my profile quite yet.

I reassured her that I hadn't been on the website since Thursday night, yet I already sensed she wanted me to 'commit' – to her. I felt slightly confused and disorientated; a feeling that I would come to know only too well.

Early on Saturday morning another message flashed-up on the screen of my mobile:

'Can I meet U this afternoon? X'

I was at home that day, finishing off some important reports. Although I *did* want to meet her, I also knew that I needed to finish my writing and I had allotted the time that day to do it. My boundaries were being tested, and I felt under pressure; I felt them being challenged. I replied to say that unfortunately, I couldn't meet her that afternoon, but I was looking forward to meeting her the following evening. In truth, that was an understatement.

Another text came through:

'Do U want me 2 go on my date with Robert 2nite?' she mused.

The feelings of jealousy returned. She was testing me again. I replied to say that as she had arranged her date before we had 'met', then the 'right thing to do' would be to do whatever she wanted, which included going on the date if she wished. I sensed that she didn't like my reply, and that she felt 'rejected' by my ambivalence.

Although my reply was 'rational', feelings of self-doubt started to flood my consciousness. Shouldn't I say 'Don't go?' 'Shouldn't I have met her after all, as she had asked?' She was drawing me in, and I could feel the conviction and belief in my own boundaries weaken.

I decided to call her later that day. I felt my heart race as I dialled the number, and I felt like it was going to explode as the call rang-out. She answered. Her; it was *her*! She was in the bath, getting ready to go on her date with Robert that evening. I heard the water in the background, and fantasised about the ripples undulating over her taught, fresh, naked body. For a moment, I wished I was the water, surrounding her very being. I felt *jealous* of the water, and wanted to reduce myself to something so simple, to touch her, and feel her. Her voice was like a symphony of light, and I felt basked in the glorious, brilliant sunshine that was 'her'.

We talked for around half-an-hour, and it confirmed my earlier feelings; she did want desperately to meet me earlier that afternoon, and I had disappointed her.

'I'm not sure that I want to meet you tomorrow after all,' she said.

Panic overcame me as I justified to her why I couldn't see her that afternoon. I gave her rational reasons why I couldn't meet her, not knowing at the time that I was engaging with someone who was devoid of rationality.

'Look, have a good time with Robert tonight. You've had this date arranged for a while, and I'll see you tomorrow?' I pleaded.

'OK, see you tomorrow then.' Relief; I managed to bring her around.

Robert was taking her to a Jazz club that evening. I didn't expect to hear from her that night, and was surprised when I did.

'Robert can't believe all the attention I get,' she boasted to me via text. 'I think he's jealous that the waiter has the hots 4 me! she continued.

If anyone was jealous, it was me. And I started to hate myself for it. Why was she sending me these texts?

I couldn't understand it at the time. But in hindsight, her narcissism was one of her 'hooks', hooks that would very soon be enmeshed with my very being; hooks that have wounded me, and scarred me for life.

Sunday afternoon couldn't come quickly enough. I nervously chose a shirt from my wardrobe, and methodically pressed the residues of my previous life from it. I wanted this shirt to be 'new'. I wanted to be 'new' myself, and reinvent myself, leaving behind all the shackles of despair and disappointment in my life. I thought that this was my chance. *My* chance to love someone whole-heartedly; to *give* myself completely to someone whom I could trust, who now knew my most intimate secrets. And I wasn't going to let her get away. My thoughts were consumed with her as I carefully dressed and ensured that I was 'good as new'.

I deserved her, I thought. I wasn't the damaged, rejected child that overwhelmed me at times. I told myself I was worthy, and I convinced myself that I deserved her love, that I could be loved in a way that I had *never* experienced before.

On that Sunday evening we'd arranged to meet for a drink in a wine bar close to where she lived.

I arrived early. Very early.

'I'm here! Wot do U want 2 drink? X' I texted impatiently. 'A large glass of Rosé please,' she replied. 'B there in 10 X'

My heart pounded as I ordered a large glass of Shiraz and a large glass of Rosé at the bar. The bartender was polite and professional. I think he sensed I was nervous. Little did he know of the ravages of emotions that were consuming me at the time. The essence of

7

Rosé wine filled my senses as I retrieved the two large glasses from the bar; flowers, the sweet aroma of a carpet of petals intoxicated me. I believed that *she* was my Rose, and my hand grasped the stem of her wineglass like I was grasping the stem of a single rose. I didn't feel the sharp thorns on the stem gouge my skin and break my physical and emotional boundaries right then; but I would later.

I sat down and waited. I glanced towards the door of the wine bar, waiting for her to arrive. Eventually, I saw a slight, delicate figure walk through the door encased in a thick coat to protect her from the February cold. I knew it was her before she even crossed the threshold. I strode over and put my arms around her, holding her just a little too long for a first meeting, embracing her slight body and feeling like I had 'come home'.

She was stunning. Her profile pictures didn't do her physical beauty justice. She removed her coat to reveal a perfectly-proportioned body covered by a simple yellow dress. Simple, uncomplicated, yet sexy and alluring. When she smiled at me that first time, *everything* in the world became perfect. We sat down at the bar, and my eyes were transfixed by her beauty. The bar was busy that evening, but everyone disappeared from my consciousness as soon as she arrived.

Our eyes became only for one-another. Her voice, her laugh were the only sounds I could hear in the busy, crowded bar that night. We talked briefly, but I have no recollection about what. Then it happened.

She slowly lowered her hand towards her side, and I caught it with mine. Shocks of lust, love and desire consumed me. I leant over to kiss her and tasted the sweet aroma of Rosé wine in her delicate, wet mouth.

My lips explored hers, and hers mine. I became hers at that point. *Completely and utterly hers.* She knew that too. She knew that I could give her what she wanted, and although I didn't know I was a 'narcissistic co-dependent' myself at that time, she knew that she wanted me, *needed me*, the moment she saw me. We didn't talk; we just kissed and immersed ourselves in one-another.

Eventually, we decided to take a walk up to a restaurant a few doors away for some dinner. We literally melted into each another as we made the brief stroll along the pavement at the edge of the dimly-lit street.

'I've never felt so safe in anyone else's arms before,' she proclaimed. Holding her, walking with her, our bodies as close as they could physically be, felt perfect.

We sat down in the restaurant, and the waitress dutifully provided us with menus. But I wasn't interested in food; I was only interested in her. My mouth became hers once more. Her hand discretely felt between my legs, and she could feel that I was physically excited by her presence. The waitress came over to take our order, and appeared uncomfortable that she was interrupting our passionate embrace. I hadn't even looked at the menu, and ordered the first thing that came into my head. I wasn't there for food, after all.

The evening flew by, both of us consumed with passion and desire. Before too soon, eleven-o-clock was approaching, and she told me she had to get back home to relieve her babysitter. Reluctantly, we made the short walk back to the wine bar where she had parked her car. We embraced on the pavement, and we couldn't bear to release one-another. Although I couldn't consciously feel them at that time, her 'hooks' were sinking into me, with every thrust of her tongue into my open mouth.

'If I hadn't parked somewhere so visible, I would let you take me now,' she whispered. 'I want to feel you inside me.'

She 'had' me. Her impulsivity that seemed so alluring to me then, would later be the cause of much pain.

When I reached home that night, I felt invincible. I impatiently booted up the PC, logged onto findyourmatch.com and suspended my profile with an assurance that I had never felt before.

I texted her: 'All sorted. Profile suspended. I'm all urs! X'

That was the start of my fateful dance with the Borderline…

Chapter 2

I was working from home the next day, so I didn't need to be anywhere; apart from with her.

I texted: 'I REALLY want 2 C U again. R U free 2nite X?'

She replied quite coolly: 'Yes. I'll cum up 2 C U at home after I finish work.'

I didn't quite understand it. Where had the woman who 'wanted' me so badly the night before gone, the woman who literally couldn't wait to meet me?

The day passed slowly, and I eventually saw her car pull up outside. I dashed to the door and embraced her, but I didn't feel the same rush of emotion from her as I had the night before; it was as if she had withdrawn from me. And I felt hurt and rejected. She wanted to talk; or rather question me. She asked me intimate details about my past relationships, which I answered honestly. I couldn't understand *why* she wanted to know so many details about my past, but I know now; she was amassing her 'arsenal' to use against me later. I reciprocated her interest in me, by asking equally probing questions, but felt a reticence from her to answer.

We ordered a take-away and we 'carried on talking', or rather she resumed her inquisition. Her hunger for information about my past was insatiable. She was testing me. After that night she knew exactly what my strengths and weaknesses were, but my weaknesses were all she was really interested in.

I went to kiss her, but she resisted. Had I done something wrong? Was it something I had said?

Later, I was to find out that it was neither. She had just felt 'engulfed' by her feelings towards me, the very love she was searching for, the love that I later found out she had failed to receive from her abusive mother as a child. And this scared her. It petrified her, because her past experiences of loving her mother caused her inordinate pain when she was abused and subsequently abandoned. The 'love' I had for her at that time scared her, because she *knew* that this would only lead to abandonment and pain. In her 'reality', there was *no* other possible outcome.

The talking came to an end, and she dropped her bombshell:

'I can't see you again. I think I still have feelings for my ex, Sean.'

I felt 'gutted' inside, as if the barbed-hooks I had allowed to penetrate my very 'being' were literally tearing my flesh apart as she retracted them. But I put on a 'brave face', held her closely as she left and wished her the best of luck.

I later found out that as soon as she left me that night, she went back to Sean and slept with him again.

Yes, they had apparently broken-up just before *we* had met the night before, but Sean wasn't *really* an 'ex'. We talked a little about him that first Monday night; about how he was still very much in-love with her, yet she admitted they had so many fundamental differences. Yvette knew deep down that the chances of forming a long-lasting relationship with him were non-existent; they were too 'different', and she could accept that.

But this realisation effectively made him emotionally 'unavailable' in her psyche, yet Yvette had a history of choosing to be with 'unavailable' partners in the past, be they physically abusive past-boyfriends in her teens, or married lovers whilst she was married.

Her 'choosing' to be with emotionally unavailable partners made her feel 'safe', because it staved-off her chronic fear of engulfment.

In contrast, she perceived me as being emotionally 'available' at that time, and her feelings of affection towards me literally scared her. She was afraid of being emotionally engulfed by those feelings, and the prospect of going back to Sean didn't scare her in the same way. In her skewed sense of 'reality', the 'safer' option was to be with someone who *didn't* make her feel engulfed.

She had bitter experiences as a child to justify, and prop-up her warped realisation of ontological existence, or of her 'being in this world', because the love she had for her abusive mother as a child *had* engulfed her, completely. And when her mother had subsequently abandoned her, this caused her great pain. In her mind, it was always 'safer' to choose someone who was emotionally unavailable, because she could then 'choose' to push them away and abandon *them* first if she wished; she could 'protect herself' in that way, and retain control over the pain she *always* associated with loving someone.

Emotionally unavailable partners were always a safer 'bet' for her. And Sean was just the latest in a long line.

Fear of 'engulfment' is the fuel that drives the Borderline psyche, and it was the basic-step of the 'dysfunctional dance' that we were starting that night...

I was being 'triangulated'. Deep down, she wanted the love that she suspected I could give her, but it scared her too much to consider receiving it. Although being with Sean was 'safer' for her at that time, she needed me on the 'sidelines', for her to pick-up and use whenever she needed me; whenever she felt *alone*. And foolishly, I was more than happy to oblige. My damaged 'inner-child' wanted her, *needed* her, even more so now that I knew she was going back to Sean.

It was with a heavy heart that I retired to my bed that night. But I was committed – committed to loving her and *making* her love me.

The next morning I dropped her a text:

'Hey, if things don't work out with Sean, let me know? U never know!? lol Keep in touch X'

I secretly hoped that things would fall apart between her and Sean as soon as possible. Then I could be retrieved from the sidelines to love her. I didn't have to wait too long. She kept in-touch via text that week, even though she was meant to be giving it 'one final go' with Sean.

It transpired that we were both in London that coming Friday on business, so I coyly suggested that we should meet for coffee in London if we were both free.

She told me she would be travelling to London on the train on Thursday night, and staying in a hotel near Euston Station that evening. I was due to get the 'red-eye' train to London first thing Friday morning.

Thursday evening arrived, and as we had yet to confirm any plans, I wasn't sure if we would be meeting in London the following day after all. I was soaking in the bath mid-evening when my mobile rang. It was Yvette.

She was distraught, and howling with psychic pain. I could almost feel the tears fall on my cheek with every cry and stuttered breath she took. Apparently, things hadn't worked out with Sean that day, and she had decided to end it – for good.

She was inconsolable, and her cries were punctuated by muffled announcements made over the carriage intercom at the various stops the train made on its way down to London. I wanted to save her. I wanted to rescue her from her pain, and if I could have transported myself onto that train at that moment in time, using every resource I had, I would have. I just wanted to hold her and take her pain away. We spoke for over an hour, in disjointed conversations in-between dark tunnels on her way to London. It was at that point that I *committed* myself to saving her, to taking away all the pain she had inside.

At the time little did I realise that her reaction had been precipitated by enforced separation between her and Sean that day. She had to go to London on Thursday to be at the Royal College for the Friday. And she was now *alone*.

This imposed separation had kicked-in her irrational fear of abandonment, and Sean was no use to her now. But I would be. She knew I would be in London the next day, and she *needed* me to fill the vacuous hole felt by the 'loss' of Sean; because he couldn't physically be there to reassure her and console her, he was thrown-away like a worn-out toy.

I couldn't wait to get the train the next morning. I hardly slept that night. I was ready; ready to be her 'knight in shining armour', her perfect partner who

15

would *never* let her down. We texted whilst I was on the train to London, back and forth. She loved texting, and her smart-phone made it so easy for her. I was later to find out that texting was her primary 'weapon', the vehicle by which she dispatched and projected her pain and self-loathing onto me.

I suspected she would be in Euston waiting for me. I had an uncanny knack of knowing her thoughts, which gave me the impression I 'knew her' – that she was my true 'Soul-mate'. My train arrived into Euston on time, and I made sure I was first at the door to exit.

Impatiently, I pushed the button for the door to open. 'Open, just open!' I found myself muttering under my breath. Eventually, the door gave way to reveal the oppressive atmosphere of diesel fumes and chatter that made Euston Station what it was. I was tall, so I could see above the sea of people dashing for the platform exit. But I wasn't looking at them. I was looking for Yvette.

As I neared the end of the platform, my heart literally melted. There she was, in all her splendid glory. Waiting; waiting for me, with a grin spreading from ear-to-ear. In a polka-dot dress that clung to her figure, demure and alluring she shone like a beacon of light, cutting through the oppressive, dark cloud in the station that day. Commuters turned and stared at her, businessmen unable to take their eyes off her, briefly distracted by a vision of beauty.

I strode quickly up to her, dropped my bags and embraced her like I have never embraced anyone else before. My mouth kissed her sweet lips, and I again tasted the soft bed of petals that I had done the Sunday evening before. We were now 'one', two people inseparable through our love and passion.

I noticed out of the corner of my eye that commuters, both men and women, were actually stopping to stare. They were busily hurrying up the ramp towards the main station concourse from the platform, but they couldn't help turn their heads and look on in amazement.

'What were they thinking?' I thought. Were they in awe at our passion, or were they jealous? 'Well, she's mine!' I thought. All mine, and no-one is going to take her away from me.

We made our way down to the taxi rank from the main station concourse, and waited in-line for a taxi, all the time embraced, just as we were on that short walk to the restaurant that Sunday evening before.

'The Royal College please,' I uttered to the taxi driver.

I knew the journey was probably only twenty minutes or so, but I wished it would last a lifetime.

Yvette played a song on her smart-phone that she had just bought. 'I'm Yours', by Jason Mraz. I couldn't think of anything more appropriate, because I *was* hers, completely. On that cold March morning in London I gave myself to her, mind, body and soul. I promised myself that I would never 'let her down' like her previous partners had done; that I would never disappoint her and that I would always be there for her.

I couldn't help notice the taxi driver's eyes stare at us in his rear-view mirror as we kissed passionately, again and again. I had arrived. I had found Nirvana. And Nirvana was Yvette.

The taxi eventually arrived at the Royal College, and we took a short stroll to the door. That day I was working quite close-by, so we agreed that we would meet-up afterwards in a pub just down from the Royal

College, have a couple of drinks and go for a meal afterwards. The day's business hung like a lead weight around my neck. But I knew that in a few short hours, I would be where I needed to be.

I arrived at the pub before Yvette. I ordered her usual glass of Rosé, and waited. She walked through the door, and I was back, back fulfilling what I now believed was my true purpose in this world. We sat and talked, then embraced and kissed. We kissed passionately, and I felt waves of love crash over me again and again. People sat at other tables in the pub were staring at us, but I didn't care. In fact, I *wanted* them to stare. I wanted them to see how lucky I was to have found something and someone that I had been searching my whole life for. We quickly finished our drinks and wandered into Convent Garden to eat.

That evening was a blur, and I would have done anything to stop the clock from moving, moving towards that inescapable time when we would have to return to Euston to catch our separate trains. We sat in a little Italian restaurant, consumed with each other. Yet again, food had little purpose, other than to act as sustenance to keep me alive so that I could continue to love this wonderful creature.

The trip back to Euston later was inevitable, but painful. How could I see her leave? Her train left before mine, so I accompanied her to the platform. I watched her take a seat in the carriage, and then watched the platform clock count closer to the minute of departure. I touched the glass of the window, and her hand reached out to mine. Two hands, previously entwined, now separated by two impenetrable double-glazed panes of glass. I stared intensely into her eyes as the train pulled out of the platform, taking my love away from me.

We had arranged that I would go over to her house the next day, so there were only a few hours of separation ahead. I found my platform and waited for my train. I reluctantly placated the demons inside me: 'It's only a few hours until I see her again,' I chanted to myself. This was something that I could rationalise at that time. After all, separation was inevitable. But I was later to discover that separation was something that Yvette could *never* cope with, something that fuelled and powered the deeply-disordered, fractured person that she was inside. If only I had known then what I know now...

For most of my adult life I had felt inadequate, 'different', and somehow unworthy. I felt like Yvette was my 'cure' for all that. She was smart, successful and sexy. She was everything a man wanted. She was the perfect package, and I felt honoured that she wanted *me*. I was later to find out that Yvette's attraction to me had more to do with my obscured, disowned emotional deficiencies that stayed with me as a core-wounded 'adult-child' walking this earth, than it had to do with any admirable traits that I had. But right at that time, on that train leaving Euston on that cold March evening, I was literally in heaven. If I had died right then, I would have died a happy man, fulfilled.

The next morning came and I could hardly contain my excitement as I drove South on the motorway to see her. Her ex-husband, Liam was picking their children up from her house first thing in the morning, so we agreed that I would arrive mid-morning. The distance of thirty-

19

five miles soon passed, with thoughts of my love for Yvette distracting me. I found her house, and rang the doorbell. There she was again, a pure vision of virginal, perfect love dressed in a long white dress that gave her the aura of an angel. To me, she was an angel. She was my saviour, from all the hurt and disappointment I had suffered in my adult life so far. She could make it all better. By loving her, I would feel worthy, worthy of a place in this world; worthy as a member of mankind.

I walked into the brightly-lit hallway, and without saying a word she gestured to me. She took my hand and slowly headed towards the stairs. She led me up the stairs like a Siren on the rocks calling out to a passing sailor: 'Come to me'. My body was shaking with excitement, and I followed her up the short flights of stairs to her bedroom. I had entered the Black Widow's lair, but I was a willing sacrifice at the time.

Our clothes fell quickly to the floor, as our bodies intertwined. Enmeshment of mind, body and soul. And I was there. Although I wasn't aware of it at the time, I was at the precipice of the 'abyss', and I was wilfully jumping in, giving myself to her and losing myself in the process.

The Siren called from the depths of the abyss, and I was determined to save her. I was her salvation, and she was mine. I promised myself that I would absorb all the pain and hurt she would ever experience, and dissipate it. I would be unfailing in my efforts to please her and make her happy, and in return she would keep me located on a high pedestal, forever elevated and 'perfect'; forever the man that I knew deep down I wasn't. But I was determined to change that. I was determined to *earn* my place as her perfect saviour. I was committed to her, and her alone.

I gave myself to her in the only way I knew how to at that time. I gave myself to her repeatedly, again and again filling her with my love. My need to give myself to her was insatiable, and so was her appetite to receive it. Sex with her that day was extraordinary. It was indescribable in its urgency, frequency and endurance. My limited emotional development at the time tricked me into thinking that this was everything I had ever wanted from life. By giving myself to Yvette in the way I had, *completely*, surely I had achieved the noblest of human endeavours – to give oneself to another without condition, and without proviso.

'Surely this is what 'sainthood' consists of?' I thought. 'Surely I could now stand in the world and take my rightful place because I had 'saved' someone from their plight, from the abyss?'

I was convinced at that time that I could rescue the Siren, that I could love her enough to save her and keep her safe from harm; that I had the strength to save *both* of us, now that I had plunged in after her. What I didn't know at the time was that this was one Siren who didn't want to be rescued, and that I had jumped in after her without a life-jacket.

In doing what I did, I lost 'myself', and the limitless power of the sea would come close to killing me. I was a breath away from drowning at the very end of our relationship nineteen-months later, but the perfect storm had only just begun...

Chapter 3

We lived apart. Thirty-five miles apart to be precise.
I knew that. But I didn't like it. I left her house on
Sunday afternoon just before her ex-husband was due to
return their children to her. After all, it was too soon to
introduce me to her young children. *Or was it?*

Already, I felt increasingly like I couldn't live
without her. I knew I had found the person I wanted to
spend the rest of my life loving. I felt like I was leaving
a part of me behind when I drove away that Sunday
afternoon. I found out much later that I was; but it turned
out to be all the fear and anger that I had repressed in
myself since childhood.

We both had busy schedules that week, but we were
intent on seeing each other again *soon*. The arrangement
she had with her ex-husband was that their children were
with him every Tuesday and Wednesday in the week,
and every other weekend. So I naturally thought that the
next time we would see each other would be on the
Tuesday. I was delighted when on Monday I received a
text from her:

'I don't very much like being on my own. Can U
come over 2nite? X'

What about the children, I thought? After a brief text
conversation we arranged that I would go over to her
house after the children had gone to bed, that we would
spend the night together, and that I would leave early
Tuesday morning before her children woke up.

I had already made arrangements to see an old friend
that Monday evening, but I cancelled those plans in a
heartbeat. I *needed* to be with her; she made me feel
'whole' like no-one had ever made me feel before.

I waited until after nine, when the kids were asleep and quietly knocked on the door. I was home again, where I 'belonged'. That night was full of passion, and I gave more and more of myself to her, piece by piece, convulsion by convulsion. She gratefully accepted it, yet never tired of taking more and more. 'How much more had I got to give?' I thought. As it turned out, I had everything I was in this world to give, everything that made me the person I was. And I was ready to give it to someone I had only known for less than a week. I was handing myself to her, piece by piece on a silver platter, saying 'Take me!' I was sacrificing *myself* for her.

I quickly sensed that my love for her became almost as important to her as the air that she breathed. However, I didn't know at that time that she couldn't 'contain' my love, and that what I was giving her *wasn't* infinite. *Or was it?*

I naively thought that eventually, if I gave Yvette enough love, it would 'save' her and we could both leave the abyss intact, together. But in reality she was a bottomless pit of despair, and no matter how much love I tried to fill her with, it would be lost in a moment of crisis. The only way I was going to get out 'alive' would be on my own. I had no idea of that then...

The next few weeks were frantic with activity. And exciting. I met her neighbours within a week, and her children within two. Creeping off in the morning before her children awoke just seemed 'wrong'. We just couldn't seem to bear being apart, and conventions about normal timescales were sidelined and ignored.

'I've brought a toothbrush and some toiletries,' I said, two-weeks into our relationship. 'That way I can spend every evening with you, and return to my house to work in the morning.' The motorway became my new familiar route to work, rather than the stairs down to my study at home.

Things were perfect, idyllic and I couldn't have wished for anything more. Then something happened, something that was to become a hallmark of our subsequent dysfunction.

It was a 'normal' Tuesday evening. Or so I thought. We'd made passionate, tender love, and fell into each other's arms. We had a 'real', almost spiritual connection that night whilst we made-love, and I felt as close to her as I had ever felt to anyone. Then I felt it again, like I had initially felt it that first Monday evening when she came to see me before returning to sleep with Sean again. She withdrew. She was cold, distant.

'What's wrong?' I asked, panicking that I had done something wrong.

She replied in a distant voice, 'I'm not sure I'm ready for this. It's too soon. I'm not sure I want it.'

My initial panic transformed into throes of fear. Was she leaving me? Didn't she want me? *But I'd given her everything! How could she not want me?* I tried to reach out to her, but to no avail. She turned her back on me in our king-sized double bed, and told me to go to sleep. She didn't want to talk to me, and was as silent now, as much as she had been vocal a few minutes earlier when she had orgasmed whilst I was deep inside her.

My chronic fear of abandonment kicked-in and my fears turned into anger. What sort of game was she playing? Was she going to leave me all alone? I felt adrenaline flood thorough my body and I felt like I wanted to 'fight or flight'. Since I had always associated fighting and anger with my dark, 'wrong' side, I decided to leave. I was scared; scared like I had never felt before. How could she contemplate leaving me all alone when I had given her absolutely everything of myself, every last drop, and every last breath? I *had* to protect myself.

I quickly dressed and scurried for the door. I was distraught, and confused. I felt rejected and 'used'. I pointed the car towards my house, and pushed the pedal.

I needed something to calm me. It was almost midnight, so I knew that I couldn't get a drink at that time. Plus, I was driving. Nicotine. Cigarettes. They would do the trick. I pulled into the twenty-four hour petrol station between her house and the motorway, bought twenty Marlboro Menthols and took a long, hard drag. The nicotine reached my brain in a few seconds, and calmed me immediately. It had been over nine-months since I had last had a cigarette. I choked on the toxic smoke as it entered deep into my lungs, confused and scared. *Why? Why had she said that?* I was angry, and I sped along the motorway towards my house, towards the place I no longer regarded as my 'home'.

My mobile phone was ringing non-stop on my way back. It was Yvette. Eight missed calls and six voicemails; all pleading with me to come back. I reached my house, chain-smoked my way through another four cigarettes and managed to fall asleep, a disturbed, tortured slumber. The mobile stopped ringing eventually.

Unwittingly, I had 'given myself' to the wrong person, a person who would in the future abuse me and attack my very being. But I loved her. And that was all I knew at that moment in time.

The dynamics of that night haunted me for the next eighteen-months of our tortuous relationship. Whilst in the relationship, I couldn't figure-out and rationalise what went 'wrong'. With distance, I now know. That night brought a fateful realisation to Yvette that she did indeed love me. That night of tender passion and love was everything she had never received from her abusive, dismissive mother. However, this made her feel 'engulfed' and scared, and although I was right by her side then, holding her, the profound love she felt for me at that precise moment in time sparked her deep-seated fear of abandonment. She 'believed' that if she loved me in the same way she had loved her mother as a young child, then surely I would leave and abandon her in exactly the same way her Mother had done thirty-years previously. Because of the abuse she suffered, she believed deep down that she was unlovable and that sooner or later I would 'discover' this 'fact' and abandon her in exactly the same way as her mother did. So her defence mechanisms were brought to the fore. And her defence mechanisms were 'pushing' people away with anger and hate. In her psyche, loving *had* to be painful. Otherwise it wouldn't be 'love'. That night she was 'pushing' me away, before I had the opportunity to 'abandon' her. 'Pushing me away' was the only way she could remain in 'control', and safeguard the fractured 'inner child' she really was inside.

A chronic fear of perceived or real abandonment is one of the characteristics of Borderline Personality Disorder, and one that would be the back-bone of our dysfunctional relationship for the next eighteen-months...

The next morning, I was feeling sorry for myself and alone. 'Had I overreacted? Surely everyone is allowed to have an off-day? My mind was telling me one thing, but my feelings were saying something else to me; and I didn't listen to them.

I called Yvette that morning to say that I would come down to see her after I had finished work. She agreed, but when I arrived, I was greeted with anger:

'If you had come back last night, it would have been very different!' she shouted.

It was obviously all my fault. I should have answered the mobile when she called. I should have gone back to her after I had left, rather than abusing myself with toxic carcinogens. I apologised. I apologised from the bottom of my heart and soul. I promised myself again that I would be there for her, in a way that no other partner had been before. I felt shame, and guilt that I had 'abandoned' her. I'd renegaded on my promise, not just to her, but to myself. I was imperfect again, a broken, 'half-a-person' without the adulation she could give me. I had slipped from that high pedestal, and needed desperately to be reinstated.

I did anything and everything I could to convince her that I deserved to put 'back on top', that it was a 'slip' of character and that it wouldn't happen again. I started to believe that if I tried harder and harder to love her, that she would never again 'feel' the things she felt the night before, *ever* again.

How wrong could I have been...?

Chapter 4

Right from the very start, sex had always been an important part of my relationship with Yvette. On reflection, it was too important. Even before we physically met on that first Sunday night, sex was bubbling under the surface. The only difference on that first night was that it came to the fore; it was explicit and 'realised' then.

I remember one of the first things she said to me on text after we met on findyourmatch.com:

'I tend 2 get alot of attention wherever I go. Is that OK with U? X'

Before we met, I already knew from her internet profile pictures that she was attractive, so I didn't think too much of it at the time. However, when she was out with her friends on the Friday night before we met, she made it very clear that men in the club she was at found her desperately attractive. And she gave exactly the same impression when she was out on her date with Robert the following night.

'Was she just insecure?' I remember thinking at the time. Was she trying to make me jealous? I must admit, at that time I did indeed feel a pang of jealousy that it wasn't me who was with her, and in flirting back with her via text in those early days, I told her so. But that's exactly what she wanted. She wanted me to feel jealousy; she was testing my 'boundaries', to see if she could penetrate them. If she could, if she could indeed instil jealousy within me before we had *even met*, then she knew that I would be a suitable 'target'; that I could potentially give myself to her 'unconditionally'.

But on the Saturday before we met, I was successful in upholding a 'boundary'. In not succumbing to pressure to meet her on that Saturday afternoon before she was due to go on her date, I instilled doubt in her mind that I would indeed be 'suitable'. Because in her mind, if I didn't 'want her' then, then surely I wouldn't 'want her' at all? That was why she came very close to cancelling our first date on the Sunday. In retrospect, I wish she had...

The night we first met, sex charged the air like the way lightening sparks in a thunderous downpour. We wanted each other, there and then. I believe that she *would* have given herself to me on that first date if she could, because she knew that sex was an effective way to lure me in. Sex was the perfect way to seduce me, and ultimately control me. And that's what sex became in our subsequent relationship; an effective way for her to control me and dictate my thoughts and actions; control my very 'being'.

When we slept together on that Saturday after we had both returned from London, I thought I was in heaven. How could I be so lucky? Here was a woman who was beautiful, intelligent, and successful *and* 'puts out' on (more or less) the first date? I thought I had met my perfect partner. That first day we made-love her appetite for sex was insatiable. I lost count of the number of times we made-love before *having* to go out for food to the local Indian restaurant in the evening, to literally prevent us 'wasting away' from hunger. I was in awe.

We never used barrier contraception right from the start. She told me that she had a coil fitted, the perfect contraceptive. I was devoid of reason when I came deep inside her, again and again that first Saturday we made-love.

But what if she had been carrying an STI? 'Surely not,' I thought. She's a doctor, and a 'respectable member of society'. In my deluded mind at the time, there was no way that she could be carrying an STI. 'And anyway,' I thought, 'she wouldn't have unprotected sex like this with just *anyone*, would she? I must be 'special', surely?' Delusion was clouding my judgement right from the very start.

Of course, I forgot at the time I was busy deluding myself that she had left me on the Monday before to sleep with her (not quite) 'ex'; I ignored the 'red flags' all along the way, because by that point I was already 'hooked'. And denial was effective in numbing the pain of her hooks that were penetrating deeper and deeper within me.

She flattered my sexual prowess with her compliments and adventurousness. She suggested that I take her anally, something I had never done before. I felt flattered that she would allow me to come inside her 'forbidden cavity'; she *wanted* me to take her, and 'abuse' her in that way.

'You're the best lover I've ever had!' she would exclaim after our marathon sex-sessions. 'No-one else can come as much as you do!'

I felt on top of the world; she was completely effective in feeding my *own* narcissism, which I needed to numb the pain of my own childhood scars. But in the end, all her compliments were just 'tools' to ensure I didn't notice her deadly hooks penetrate deeper and deeper.

Throughout our relationship, she always said we that 'fucked like bunnies.' Sex was frequent and plentiful right up until the very end. Sometimes we would make love several times a day; whenever we could. We used to laugh about the fact that my juices would always be dripping into her knickers when she left for work in the morning. In the 'honeymoon' period of our relationship sex helped reinforce, in her mind, that I did indeed love her. And at the time, I was all too willing to oblige. Orgasm for me was a natural release, and a way to show her that I did indeed love her. And because we were having unprotected sex right from the start, I was fooled into believing that she must 'trust' me; after all, it could have been *me* carrying an STI rather then her. But she never did 'trust' me, because deep down she never had the capacity to truly 'trust' herself.

A little while into our relationship, after the honeymoon period had passed, I started to notice a few 'red flags' connected with our sex life. I sensed that she was very keen for me to orgasm, but that she didn't orgasm as frequently or as easily. I wondered why. After all, to a chronic co-dependent like me, it was important that she 'enjoyed' sex too. In fact, her enjoyment from sex became more important than my own fulfilment.

We discussed this one day, and she said 'As long as you orgasm, then I'm happy.' I felt disappointed, that she didn't orgasm as frequently or as easily.

I'm not a sexologist, but I thought I knew about the different types of orgasm a woman could experience; and I wanted Yvette to experience them all. One day I went to 'go down on her', to give her oral sex in a bid to provide her with an orgasm. To my surprise, she pulled away. I couldn't understand it.

32

I felt a little rejected, and jokingly said 'I didn't realise you were so sexually inhibited?' In response, she raged at me. I had insulted her and undermined her inner 'Self', and she didn't let me forget about that incident for a long time to come.

She had a vibrator, and she loved it as most women probably do. She was thrilled that I was happy to use it as part of our love-making.

'Most other men feel 'threatened' by it. I'm so glad you enjoy using it with me,' she enthused.

But I started to notice that the vibrator became a major part of her climb towards orgasm. She dissuaded me from physically stimulating her clitoris with my fingers whilst I was penetrating her. And it was all about control. She *had* to remain in control over when and how she orgasmed, in order that she could stave off her feelings of engulfment that the loss of control associated with an orgasm is associated with. She couldn't really 'let go' in our sex life, and to do so would have precipitated feelings of engulfment, and subsequent abandonment.

I came to realise this after we had had 'make up' sex. As the cycles of dysfunction started to rear their ugly heads later in our relationship, we would often participate in extremely passionate, all-consuming love-making after we had argued. At those times, she would readily orgasm vaginally when I was deep inside her. But immediately afterwards, she would withdraw, in a similar way to that Tuesday night I had deserted her after we had finished making passionate love.

In essence, by losing control of herself, she felt threatened that her love for me would engulf her very 'being'. And her childhood experiences with her mother taught her one thing: that to love someone *completely*, meant that they *would* abandon her, in the same way her own mother had. She withdrew after particularly passionate love-making because she feared that I would do exactly what her mother did; *leave* her. Therefore, she 'pushed me away' emotionally before I could 'abandon' her first. She *had* to remain in control at all cost.

A little later in our relationship, our sex life went through a bit of a 'dry patch'. That's probably quite natural for any couple. At the time, I remember I was particularly stressed at work and my libido suffered. It had been about a week since we had last made-love.

'You obviously don't love me anymore, do you?' she accused.

I couldn't understand her at that time, and I became angry. 'Of *course* I love you!' I reassured her.

I explained that I felt particularly stressed with work, and that it was just a natural cycle in any relationship. But that I did indeed love her, with all my heart and soul. In response, she became angry and defensive.

'You think I'm ugly and unattractive, don't you?' she screamed.

This was her fractured, inner-child speaking. And yet again, as with any outward expression associated with perceived abandonment, she was attempting to project all her deep-seated pain and self-loathing onto me.

On one level, sex with Yvette was fulfilling; on a superficial, physical level I enjoyed my orgasms immensely and appreciated her willingness to receive them. But ultimately our love-making lacked any real depth, intimacy and 'safety'. Sex was always on 'her terms', and hers alone. I started to increasingly think that our sex life resembled sex with a shallow 'porn-star', someone two-dimensional; a 'cardboard cut-out' of a sexual partner.

And to all intents and purposes, she fitted that bill exactly. She was attractive and 'sexy', and because of her Borderline characteristics, she did indeed lack emotional development. And as a damaged adult-child myself, I did too.

Sex with Yvette felt like I 'thought' it should have at that time, because I wasn't allowing myself to 'feel'; my *own* childhood experiences impacted not only on being unable, in a 'self-censuring' way, to feel 'negative' feelings of anger and revolt; but they were also responsible for muting any *true* feelings of elation and joy. The 'yin-yang' of my emotional 'palette' was lacking, making the 'reds' of passion and desire completely useless and nonsensical without being able to feel the 'blues' of melancholy and anger. I too was as emotionally 'two-dimensional' as Yvette. We were indeed 'made for each other', both inside and outside the bedroom.

In the end, and even at the start of our relationship, sex was all about 'control'. It was a useful way that someone with Borderline 'Waif' characteristics like Yvette could manipulate and retain their 'captor'. However, because of my own stunted emotional development at that time, I was more than a willing prisoner; I locked the door *myself* and threw away the key…

It was a Saturday, a few weeks into our relationship. After we had made-love in the morning, we had arranged for the neighbours to come around, and we were planning to be the perfect hosts. For the first time in my life I felt accepted as 'whole' by Yvette, and by her friends and neighbours. Her neighbours were lovely, 'normal' people from middle-class families; just the sort of people I felt comfortable with. Yvette was 'queen' of the kitchen. By that point, we had pretty much worked out a 'system'. She was 'Chief Cook', took charge of cooking for us, and I was 'Chief Clearer-up', doing everything I could to aid and abet her in the creation of her culinary masterpieces. And she was a good cook.

By mid-afternoon the kitchen was crowded with neighbours, and adult conversation was drowned-out by the screams of happy children playing. We had decided, or rather Yvette had decided that the young children would be eating pizza for dinner. I removed the pizza from the oven after the cooking-time had elapsed, but it wasn't quite ready. I informed Yvette that it needed a little longer, and she agreed. A few minutes later she asked me to remove the pizza from the oven but I told her that it probably needed a little longer, and that as she was busy entertaining, to leave it to me. I should have listened.

A few minutes later I retrieved the pizza from the oven to find that one-half had been slightly overcooked. Feelings of disappointment overcame me. I had let her down, again.

'I told you that it would be burnt by now!' she snapped. There was a look of distain in her eyes, one that I would grow to recognise, and in time normalise. I offered to eat the overcooked section, but it had already happened; I had fallen yet again from that pedestal I so coveted. I was, yet again, devalued and dismissed.

The look of distain and disgust in her eyes that day awoke familiar feelings from my childhood. When she

glanced at me in that way and spoke to me in the way
she did, I was immediately transported back to being
five years-old again; to a relationship that had shaped the
very person I was - my childhood with my abusive
Mother.

Chapter 5

For many years, my life as a child remained a mystery. Before I met Yvette, I was of the opinion that I had quite a 'normal' upbringing, full of love from my (admittedly) imperfect parents. I was the eldest child of a family of four. My parents married young, and my mother fell pregnant quite quickly. She gave birth to a stillborn little girl, a year or so before I came along. I was born in nineteen-sixty-nine, one of the last children of the hedonistic sixties, and a few weeks before Neil Armstrong set foot on the moon. My brother came along a couple of years later, and our 'family' was complete.

I don't remember too much about my early childhood. We moved around a great deal, in response to my Father's whimsical (but ultimately unsuccessful) career. We settled in the North of England in my 'formative' years, but I started to suspect that something was 'wrong' in my childhood. My mother was a very volatile person. She had excessive mood-swings and I could never predict what sort of 'mood' she would be in from day-to-day.

When I was eight, I remember finding tablets in her bathroom cabinet. A curious little child, I was exploring the world around me, and this little smoked-brown container held things I hadn't seen before: 'What was Lithium?' I remember thinking to myself.

My mother and father had a very volatile, conflictual relationship. I remember the times that my mother used to rage at my father in front of me, in our small council-owned flat.

I have some memories. My mother had bought my father a lovely watch for his birthday one year, one of those self-winding ones that probably cost more money than they could really afford. My father requested that my mother return it. I'm not sure of the reason why he suggested this, but in response my mother erupted into a fit of rage.

'Nothing I buy that man is *ever* good enough!' she shouted in front of me.

In these formative years, my father was distant and aloof. He worked in the motor industry, and worked long hours. He was early out-of-the-door in a morning, late home at night, and often absent at weekends. He was my father, but I never really felt like he was 'there' for me. I can't remember a single day when he solely devoted his time and attention to me as a young child, where he took an active interest in what *I* wanted to do. As long as I was doing well at school, he was happy. Or at least he seemed it.

My relationship with my mother was very different. In the relative absence of my father, my mother became the primary 'caregiver' in my life. She was home when I returned from school; she baked cakes for me to gorge myself on when I returned home hungry. And she beat and abused me.

My mother's abuse towards me started at an early age. Maybe I *had* been bad, but I still remember the sting on my bottom, and the pain of trying to sit down after she had almost broken the skin on my tender, young bottom. The beatings became more severe as I grew older, into my 'formative' years. Her hand was soon replaced by the sole of a 'Scholl' sandal as I grew in size. My physical growth seemed to be proportionately linked to the severity of the beating I received; the bigger I grew, the bigger beating I received.

Trying to predict and 'guess' when these beatings were going to happen was like trying to predict the outcome of the National Lottery. When I returned from school, I *hoped* that she would be in a 'good' mood, and that I would be praised and fed chocolate cake. But more often than not, I returned home to find her emotionally dysregulated and violent; and I knew what was coming next.

I remember rushing home as quickly as I could, to ensure that I was the first through the door, ahead of my brother.

'Better she beat me, rather than him,' I thought. I had to protect him.

And I had to 'look after' my violent mother. I tried everything I could to ensure a 'good' outcome. I can still recall the feelings of trepidation as I put my key in the lock of the front door, not knowing what lay behind. Was she going to be in a good mood, or not? How hard would she hit me? Would she stop after three blows, or ten?

I was 'walking on eggshells' with my mother for all of my childhood life, and whenever I was beaten I *always* thought it was 'my fault'. It was my fault that I didn't look after her properly, that I didn't love her enough. Surely, if I loved her 'more' she would stop doing this to me? And obviously I deserved what I got. I was a bad, despicable person deep inside, and I thought I deserved every blow, every wince of pain I felt from that sandal. I was worthless as a person, and my mother reinforced that notion within me at every opportunity.

41

I was an average student at school, but I worked hard. It seemed the only way to gain approval from my emotionally and physically absent father, and my enraged mother. Surely if I did well at school, she would stop hitting me and love me in the way I wanted her to love me? I didn't know what I wanted to do with my life, but I felt I *needed* to escape. I didn't want to be beaten, but I wasn't sure of how to stop it. Obviously I deserved the beating, or so I thought. So therefore, I must make myself a 'better' person; a person that other people would see as 'good' and worthy.

The birth of my own narcissistic tendencies had just been instilled within me...

It was nineteen-seventy-eight. I was nine years-old. I had just discovered music. And I loved it. I remember the feeling of excitement when I received a cassette-tape with the soundtrack of 'Saturday Night Fever' recorded on it as a Christmas present. I was obviously way too young to see the film itself at that time. It was an 'X' Certificate; eighteens only. But I was fascinated by the character of Tony Manero, played in the film by the great John Travolta. Here was a man who rebelled against his oppressive parents, and did what 'he wanted to do'. And he found freedom in dance and music, just as I wanted to do.

I was thrilled when the film studio brought out an 'A' Certificate of the film, and I hounded my parents to take me to see it. Tony Manero was a 'god', and probably always will be. I wanted to be like him. I wanted to be able, like him, to rebel against my parent's oppression.

My father had a brother who was much younger. There was a large age-gap. At that time he had just returned from University, with a relatively poor degree from a relatively poor University. But he had music. He possessed a 'proper' Pioneer stereo, with big Wharfedale speakers, and a tape-deck with moving needles and lights. It was heaven. He was more like a big brother to me than an uncle. And I still credit him with introducing me to music. The Eagles, Linda Ronstadt, Billy Joel and ABBA. They were all there on my uncle's stereo, and I was in heaven. He was also the one who recorded me the 'Saturday Night Fever' soundtrack on that cassette-tape that I almost wore out. And of course, the Bee Gees were a big part of that soundtrack.

In nineteen-seventy-nine the Bee Gees brought out an album called 'Spirits Having Flown'. Their falsetto harmonies made me happy, and I saved all of my pocket money for weeks to buy this album on cassette-tape. Eventually, I managed to save up enough money to buy a copy, and I still remember the day I opened that little cassette box with anticipation and delight.

Christmas was approaching, and my brother wanted a cassette-player to play his music on. My parents bought him a Ferguson radio-cassette, which allowed me to play my music too. We shared a bedroom at that time, and I appreciated the joy this little box of transistors gave me.

By this time, my parents had made some friends in the local area. At the time my mother worked in a haberdashery shop in the local shopping precinct, and she became friendly with one of the customers. Her friend used to come into the shop to buy wool, and very soon they were socialising as a 'foursome'; my parents, my mother's friend and her husband called Steven.

At Christmas-time in nineteen-seventy-nine we were all invited around to their house for a get-together, and my brother took his new radio-cassette player for music. I also took my new Bee Gees cassette to play. Whilst the music played and our parents danced, I noticed something strange. My mother appeared overly 'intimate' with Steven, and when they danced to the music they seemed a little bit 'too' close. When they asked that I repeat the track 'Spirits Having Flown' from the album, they danced even closer. I knew something was wrong.

We moved house two years later in nineteen-eighty-one, a few miles from the council estate we were previously living at. My father had tried hard to give up smoking, they had raised a deposit and bought their first home together in the era of Thatcherite home ownership. Steven was a frequent visitor to the house, and would often 'call in' to see my mother on his own. He was always friendly and 'made a fuss' of me and my brother, something absent from my relationship with my father. But I suspected that my mother and him were 'too close', and my fears were soon to be realised.

One Friday evening, my father was out with his brother and brother-in-law for their usual Friday-night drinking session. My mother was home alone, and Steven called around. My brother and I were soon dispatched to bed, but I knew something wasn't quite right. I crept down the stairs from my bedroom, on the premise of recovering some money from the mantelpiece; I opened the door to the lounge and found them there, tightly embraced in a passionate kiss on the sofa in the pitch-black darkness. I was hysterical. How could my mother do this to my father? *How could she cheat on him?* I ran back to my bedroom, tears falling down my face. I had discovered the truth I had suspected all along; my mother and Steven were having an affair. I was inconsolable. My mother stormed into my bedroom, trying desperately to change my perception of reality:

'You've been watching too much Dallas!' she screamed at the top of her voice.

It didn't matter what she said. I *knew* what was going on.

Her assertiveness turned to rage, and she tried to emotionally beat the knowledge that I now had out of me. She invalidated my feelings, in exactly the same way she used to do with her Scholl sandal.

'Don't you dare tell your father!' she screamed.

How could I tell my father? If I did there would be hell to pay, and I would be the one paying it. How could I trust my feelings and emotions after that point? My primary caregiver was telling me that I was 'wrong' to feel what I did, that I *had* to succumb to her parental superiority. I was broken, and from that day I hived off all the pain and anger I felt towards her, in order that I could continue to love her. I *needed* to love her; but I also needed to leave her.

I was sixteen when I returned home from school one day; the day I became Tony Manero and 'became a man'. My mother went for me, to hit me around the face. But I was bigger and stronger than her now. I grasped the arms of her diminutive body as she went to strike me. I stopped her, and held on tight.

'NO Mother, stop it!!' I shouted.

I will never forget the look of rage in her eyes at that time. It will stay with me until the day I die, and it came back to haunt me twelve-years later.

I left home as soon as I practically could, away from my abusive caregiver, but was left with a sense of failure. I was 'running away'; I wasn't Tony Manero after all. I didn't rebel. I left on the premise of pursuing a University education, a great distance from her.

But I felt like I had deserted my mother, and had 'failed' to look after her; I had failed to *make* her love me. And it was an experience that would haunt me for the rest of my adult life.

Christmas, nineteen-ninety-seven. Twelve years later. I was at my mother's house for Christmas, with my two young children, aged two-years and one-year. Nappies everywhere, and the constant smell of used nappy sacks lingered in the air. My wife was at her father's that Christmas, because he was alone that year. My brother also joined us for Christmas at my mother's house. We sat down for Christmas lunch. My two year-old son was in a playful mood. He was licking his uncle sat next to him, and laughing with delight. My brother was playful and tender, reciprocated and laughed along with him.

Speaking directly to my son, my mother balled 'Stop that now, Sam!' at the top of her voice.

'Mum, he's fine,' I said. 'He's only having a laugh with his uncle.' I thought that would be the last of it. I was there as his father, and I deemed his conduct to be appropriate for a normal two year-old.

The rage that I remember seeing in her eyes when I stopped her hitting me twelve years ago appeared again that day; an incontrollable urge to punish and control.

'Sam, STOP that now! I mean it!' she screamed. The look of anger in her eyes transported me straight back to that time when I had 'become' Tony Manero.

'No Mother, shut up! He's fine, so *leave him alone!*' There was no way that I would allow a child of mine to be abused in the same way that I was at her hands.

After that, I collected my family together and left as soon as I practically could. In the weeks that followed, I offered my mother an apology for what I said to her that Christmas day. But I also requested an apology from her, to help me gain acceptance in this world that I was indeed an 'adult' deserving of respect and love, as not just her son, but as a father in my own right. No apology was forthcoming, and we didn't speak for eight years. And in those eight years, the marginalised, underdeveloped 'adult' within me felt justified that I had protected my precious son from the abuse that I had suffered as a child. But the 'inner child' within me felt like a failure, that I had yet again failed to make my mother love me.

My wife and I divorced at the very end of the period I excommunicated my mother from my life. My son was now ten. And I felt responsible for yet another broken family roaming this earth. Although I didn't recognise it at that time, I thought I was destined to roam this world as a 'core-damaged' adult-child, always searching for the love my mother never gave me. And I thought meeting Yvette was my salvation from annihilation; *she* became my saviour.

I didn't know it at the time, but attempting to love Yvette would bring me far more pain than attempting to love my mother *ever* brought me…

Chapter 6

We were three-months into our relationship. I knew that Yvette could be 'moody' and unpredictable at times, but I was convinced I could make her love me. I was convinced that _this_ time, I would be a 'success'.

Although I didn't realise it at the time, our relationship felt like an 'old pair of slippers'. These 'slippers' weren't really any use in protecting your feet like slippers should, but they felt comfortable and familiar. We had relational dynamics that, in retrospect, reminded me of my relationship with my mother. Yvette was effectively my mother incarnate; and I was increasingly 'committed' to making her love me.

We both had leave to take from work, so I suggested to her that we both go away on holiday. We hadn't been on a holiday yet, and I thought the time together would allow us to become closer; it would give me time to _convince her_ that I did love her, and to reassure her that my love for her was 'real'.

I happened upon a cheap deal to Egypt, in a five-star all-inclusive resort. I'd never been to Egypt before, and neither had she. To be honest, I didn't care where we went, as long as we were together; as long as I had exclusive time with her to love her, and _make_ her love me. She was thrilled.

'Egypt! Wow!' she exclaimed. 'Yes,' I replied. 'I can't wait!'

The grim June morning we left London behind transformed, through a long-haul flight, into a glorious Egyptian sunset. We were there at last, together.

The first few days of our hedonistic week together were idyllic. We made-love in every possible place in the resort, and we immersed ourselves in one-another. She was the perfect picture of beauty, and I was firmly attached to the top of that pedestal yet again. I thought at the time that I couldn't fall; that I had secured my place there forever. I started to believe that she would love me forever; that my place in her heart was incontrovertibly secure.

In the morning we ate and made-love, and in the afternoon we took Salsa lessons on the beach. A perfect week. I think she quite liked the fact that the Salsa teacher found her attractive, and at the time I thought I was secure enough in my love for her that his preoccupation with her amused me; it played to my own narcissistic tendencies. But she was mine; *all mine*.

The weather in the resort changed towards the end of the week. The constant sun was replaced by wind and rain, and the Salsa class one day was held indoors. Apart from a change in venue, there was also a change in the teacher. The replacement teacher didn't seem to give her quite the same attention she had so hungrily lapped-up in the preceding days, and she seemed annoyed. After the class that day we decamped to the pool for a drink, but she seemed distracted and on-edge.

I ordered some drinks, but was shocked when out-of-the-blue she said:

'You don't really love me do you, you just want to *own* me don't you!?'

I was dumbfounded. *Of course I loved her*. I loved her with all of my heart and soul! At that point in time, I loved her more than I loved myself. She remained distant, and she asked that I buy her some cigarettes. 'Cigarettes? But she doesn't smoke?' I thought. I was frustrated and angry. I tried to reassure her that I did indeed love her, and that she doesn't want to smoke.

I knew at that time she went through a brief period in the past when she did smoke, when she had a brief lesbian relationship after she had left her first husband, but she was a doctor for goodness sakes! Why would she dream of smoking?

She stormed off and 'wanted to be alone'. I let her go, and found the hotel lobby where there was a shop. I prayed they sold cigarettes. They weren't for Yvette – they were for me. I bought twenty Marlboro Lights, went back to our room and sat on the outside terrace, smoking one after another.

'Why was she like this?' I asked myself. At the time I didn't have the answers.

I heard the door open about an hour later. She walked in and didn't say a word.

'I've got your cigarettes,' I said, hoping for some response. There was none.

We showered in silence, and dressed to go out that evening. We had booked an evening at the Italian restaurant in the complex, a place we had been before. The food there was divine, and bookings were hard to secure. We sat in silence for the first two courses. I tried to make conversation, but felt rebuffed at every attempt. I felt that familiar feeling of anxiety rise within me, and felt rejected and spurned. In-between the second and third courses she finally uttered a sentence:

'I don't think we're going to work, are we?'

My anxiety turned to rage, as I stood up and threw my napkin on the table. 'Fine!!' I shouted, and hastily exited the restaurant, slamming the door behind me.

My own core issues of abandonment had been triggered again. I was convinced that Yvette was going to leave me. And I felt a failure because of it. Toxic guilt and shame overcame me, and I needed a 'solution' *now*. I headed for the bar. 'Triple whiskey on the rocks,' I ordered. Then another. Then another.

The bartender eventually said 'Would you like the bottle instead Sir?' smirking to his co-worker from the side of his face. I knew then that I had to return; I had to return to my nemesis, hopefully a-slumber in our room.

I stumbled back to our room, unsure as to what reception I would receive. I felt like that little boy again, turning the key in the lock when I got home from school all those years ago, unsure as to whether my mother would beat me. I saw her slight body, still, under the covers. She was asleep; I wasn't going to get 'beaten' tonight after all.

I saw the diamond necklace I gave her on the anniversary of out first month together discarded by the sink like a cheap trinket. It wasn't the first and last time that this would be removed from her neck, an undying symbol of my love for her, discarded when she didn't feel my love anymore.

I lay beside her and slept a few tortured hours, unsure as to what my reception would be the following morning...

The morning came, and the sun shone again. But it did nothing to alleviate my mood. There was a Jacuzzi-bath in our room, and I filled it with hot water for us to bathe. Yvette eventually stirred, and reluctantly, silently, joined me in the bath.

There was *nothing* else I could do; I broke down emotionally whilst feeling warm and safe in the warm water, and at that moment gave her the last bit of me that was keeping me alive: my insecurities about being abandoned, and being loved. She held me, put her arms around me and at long last 'loved me' in just the way I *needed* to be loved.

I told her, through a flood of sobbing tears, that I was convinced that she would leave me one day, convinced that she would see me for the person I believed I was deep down; the despicable, worthless person that my mother had beaten when I was a child.

I had now given myself to her completely, and any weak 'boundaries' that I possessed prior to that morning were now in tatters. I trusted her with my deepest, darkest secret. I trusted her to take that insecurity and cherish it; to 'look after me' in the same way I had promised to look after her.

In the end, she used it against me; she used this deep-seated insecurity to persecute me and torture me during the remainder of our relationship, reinforcing my feelings of worthlessness that were formed within me as a result of the abuse I experienced as a child.

Yvette was a damaged 'adult-child' herself, and the only way she could alleviate her pain was to prey on someone weaker and control them. And I was only too willing to accommodate her, because I believed that I *deserved* this. I didn't believe I deserved any better, any better than the pain I had experienced all my life in trying to love my mother, and now in trying to love Yvette.

With distance, I'm able to rationalise what happened that day in Egypt. Yvette was pathologically narcissistic, which is a fundamental characteristic of the Borderline personality. I too had my prosaic narcissistic tendencies, but hers were needed to reinforce and bolster her fragile sense of 'Self', and the constant 'feeding' of her narcissistic hunger was essential in order for her to maintain the delicate integrity of her very 'being' in this world. Narcissism was *imperative* to her, in order to support her very ontological existence. Without it, she would 'crumble' and literally experience a crisis in her very *identity*.

The Salsa class being indoors that day was a 'trigger'. She was disappointed and she showed it. The absence of the regular Salsa teacher that day, who adored her, was a further trigger. He functioned as a suitable 'triangulator', someone who adored and worshipped her as much as I did. And she knew it.

She always needed a point of triangulation, which ranged from an 'unavailable' Salsa teacher, to remaining in touch with an old lover whom she had had an affair with whilst in her first marriage. This liaison with her old lover persisted throughout the course of *our* relationship, until he died in a tragic road-traffic accident at the end of our relationship. I don't think it was coincidental that the physical death of her old lover signalled the true death of *our* relationship some eighteen-months later; she no longer had someone to triangulate with. And she needed that, in case I 'abandoned her'. In that way there would always be someone else to make her feel worthy, to make her feel loved. And her continued liaison with him simultaneously prevented her feeling 'engulfed' by *my* love, and her love for me; there was *always* an 'escape route' from that for her - through her continued relationship with her ex-lover.

That day in Egypt she felt 'triggered', bored and unloved. To feel love, she had to feel pain. So she 'acted out' and vented her dysregulated feelings and emotions by saying that I didn't really love her, and that I only wanted to 'own' her.

She knew at the time that it would exacerbate my own insecurities and bring my own fears of abandonment to the surface. She knew that in response I would 'leave her' emotionally, which precipitated the pain she associates with love; the only way she knew *how* to love.

At that point in time, I was so enmeshed with her that I started to question my own perception of reality.

'Was it me?' 'Surely I can try harder to reassure her that I love her?'

But it was going to get much, much worse before it would get better...

Chapter 7

As the summer-solstice came and went, and the temperatures outside soared, Yvette's birthday was approaching. I was excited, and I was determined to make this one, her 'first' birthday celebration of our relationship, one to remember.

She said that her second ex-husband, Liam had always made a big fuss over birthdays, which appeared to bemuse and annoy her slightly. As I was very soon to find out, the *truth* was that it was *her* who needed to make a big fuss over birthdays, especially her own.

Projection of her narcissism, and all of her other deep-seated, self-loathing characteristics that she so hated, became her primary mode of survival. And although Liam was a suitable 'receptacle' at that time in our relationship for the projection of her self-loathing, as our enmeshment deepened, they were very soon to be projected onto me instead.

With retrospect, trying to appreciate Yvette's 'truth' was like being lost in a dark-hall, filled with distorting fairground mirrors. An accurate representation of her 'truth' was impossible to 'find', because she didn't really know what it was herself. Apart from not knowing her own 'truth', she didn't even know her 'Self', and for far too long over the coming months I became lost in that hall of horrors, trying to find an accurate reflection, a picture of her reality.

I planned her birthday meticulously. A present. I needed a present. I decided to buy her a pair of diamond earrings to match her necklace that I had bought for her a few months earlier; the necklace that was periodically discarded when she didn't feel that I loved her.

'Oh, they're lovely!' the shop assistant in the jewellers remarked, as she carefully gift-wrapped them for me. 'I'm sure that whoever the lucky-lady is, she will be thrilled with these,' she went on. I hoped that Yvette would indeed be thrilled, but I would soon discover it would be the complete opposite.

I booked a table at the restaurant where we first ate on that intoxicating Sunday night we first met. We hadn't been back there together since, so I thought it would be fitting to revisit the birth-place of our passion. I'd picked a time when all our children could be with us together; I wanted this to be a real family celebration.

I'd already got her eldest son, Christopher, to sign a birthday card to 'Mummy', and had even managed to get her youngest son to add his scribbled 'autograph'. My own children were excited too, and transcribed their heart-felt best wishes into their own cards. They were also thrilled to be going out to a 'posh' restaurant, all together as a family.

Everything was 'set'. I hadn't told Yvette where we were planning to go, even though she pestered me to tell her. 'She's going to love it,' I thought to myself.

As the restaurant was only a five-minute drive from her house, we decided to 'buck' with convention and squeeze into one car. As I drove, her youngest son bounced on my daughter's lap in the back-seat, gurgling to himself. I felt like we were a perfect family, going out for a perfect evening.

She was thrilled to see the route I was taking, and had already guessed where we were headed for.

'Oh, thank-you Darling!' she screamed with delight. 'It's going to be lovely, and I love you so much. You're my hero!' she proclaimed as she kissed me on the cheek.

Well, I was her hero at that minute in time, but I would only remain on that pedestal for another sixty more precious minutes as it would turn out.

The restaurant that evening was filled with other families taking-in an early dinner, and the atmosphere was buzzing with delight. We decided to order main-courses straight away, as everyone was hungry, and her boys were becoming a little fractious with impatience. The food was lovely. We all gave Yvette our cards, and told her how much we loved her.

'Happy birthday Darling,' I whispered in her ear as I gave her the small box that was so perfectly gift-wrapped. She opened it, and her eyes widened with delight. She loved them, and immediately proceeded to place them in her perfectly-formed ears.

Things were perfect, but they didn't stay that way for very much longer.

With main-courses eaten, discussion turned to desserts. The waiter enthusiastically brought over dessert menus for us all to choose from. The children were busy deciding whether they wanted ice-cream or chocolate cake. And then she 'turned', and I felt myself slipping, yet again.

She stopped talking. She withdrew. And I knew something was wrong.

'What do you fancy for dessert Darling?' I tentatively enquired.

'Nothing. I want to go home,' she replied.

'But the children all want desserts?' I beckoned to the menu, trying desperately to cling-on to my pedestal.

But in her eyes, I was already on the floor, bleeding from the impact of the fall. I was just a useless pile of bleeding flesh and broken bones that was of no use to her now; just a blood-soaked inconvenience on the landscape her psyche, an ugly 'eyesore' that she needed to erase *now*.

'Can we have the bill please?' she barked at the waiter.

My children looked confused.

'Daddy, I thought we were having dessert?' my daughter pleaded with me. 'I think we're going home instead Darling,' I replied, confused, disorientated and hurt.

We left the restaurant without speaking; or rather, without her speaking to me. The children really did want ice-cream, so she reluctantly agreed to call into the local supermarket a few doors down from the restaurant, to satisfy the children's craving for frozen cream and sugar.

'What's wrong Darling?' I asked her in the supermarket aisle.

No reply. I went to put my arm around her, but I was violently rebuffed. 'What have I done wrong?' I thought. I felt dejected and alone.

The short trip home felt a million times longer than the one we took only a couple of hours earlier. As this was a 'school night', I had arranged with my ex-wife that I would return my children to her after the meal. On returning from the restaurant, I bundled my children into the back of my car and headed up the motorway, still dazed and confused.

By the time I got back to Yvette's later, her children were in bed. And she still wasn't talking to me.

I walked into the kitchen to see her necklace and earrings, purposely positioned on the kitchen side, discarded yet again. I became angry. I *knew* what that symbolic gesture meant by now.

'Yvette, just what the hell is wrong? I pleaded, trying desperately to control and suppress my anger, just like I had done for the whole of my life.

'You couldn't even be arsed to organise a cake, could you, you useless bastard!'

What? A *cake*? I couldn't believe what I was hearing. In a desperate attempt to 'save myself' I cried: 'The kids were all looking forward to dessert. Why did we need a cake?'

'No!' she replied angrily, 'Christopher was disappointed there wasn't a birthday cake for his Mummy, and it's all your fault!'

I didn't know what to say. I *knew* that Christopher was more than happy to choose a dessert from the restaurant's menu, and I hadn't noticed even a tinge of disappointment in him at any time during that evening.

'Just GO! Just fuck-off and LEAVE! she screamed.

Devastated and hurting, I retrieved my car keys and made the fifth journey that same day up that familiar stretch of motorway. I couldn't 'figure it out'; I couldn't understand her. I was lost, yet again in that dark hall, full of distorted reflections.

The events of that night were just a replay of what happened in Egypt just a short month earlier. Her pathological narcissism had got the 'better' of her yet again.

Her reaction to the lack of a cake that night had nothing to do with Christopher's 'disappointment' because he *wasn't* disappointed. Her son was perfectly happy that evening. Yvette's extreme reaction was just the total projection of her *own* disappointment onto me.

That night was the night I *became* the 'receptacle'
for her self-loathing, rather than her ex-husband Liam.
She had now found a new 'depository' – me. And I
became that receptacle because at that point in time she
believed that I would *never* leave her; she had tested my
personal 'boundaries' and was now confident that I
would accept everything she needed to 'project' onto
me.

And I no longer had any boundaries to 'protect' my
'Self'. I now 'belonged' to her.

Yvette *loved* being the centre of attention; a
narcissist in the truest sense. She *needed* to experience a
public display of adulation connected with her birthday,
involving cake, candles and the rest of the restaurant
around us that night in order to bolster her fragile,
damaged sense of 'Self'. Adulation and attention from
'strangers', such as from the restaurant staff and other
diners was as important to her as any attention and love
that her 'family' around her could give her.

Because I hadn't arranged for a cake at the restaurant
that evening, she felt let-down and emotionally
abandoned; in exactly the same way she felt when her
mother abandoned her as a young child. Her fractured
'inner-child' was 'venting' again, pushing away the
person whom she held 'responsible' for that pain, the
person whom she was deep-down too 'scared' to love;
me.

That was the last of her birthdays we spent together.
On her birthday the following year, she would be
sleeping with someone else, and trying desperately to
'move on' from me. I shouldn't have known that fact,
either at the time itself, or later. But I would know.

And I think you probably know by now the reason why I would…

Chapter 8

Life after that first birthday was turbulent. Yes, there were good times, times when we 'came together' and spent all weekend in bed making love; times when I was adored and idolised, like I had been in the first throes of our relationship. And I needed that idolisation more and more, like a drug; just like a 'junkie' after his next 'fix', I would do *anything* to ensure that I remained aloft my pedestal.

But to stay there, and unbeknown to me at the time, I was constantly 'walking on eggshells'. Her unconscious mind became mine; her unconscious concerns became *mine*; and I consciously decided that the purpose of my life was to live for her and her alone.

I was toxically enmeshed, and I had no way out. But at the time I didn't want 'out'. Far from it. I became complicit in my 'capture', and a willing hostage for her. I wanted to be there, to love her so that she would love me in return. I made excuses for myself, and committed to 'trying harder', for *her*.

Whilst in my relationship with Yvette, my behaviour and my 'way of being' changed. I stopped using underarm deodorant because she said the aerosol gave her a headache.

One day I forgot, to be met with her barking '*I thought I told you that I didn't like that deodorant! It gives me a headache!*'

Before the particles of aluminium-oxide had the chance to disperse themselves from the bathroom to the bedroom where she was laid, she was already demanding that I bring her Paracetamol. My penance for disobedience.

Yvette had a constant plethora of physical ailments that I just couldn't understand. Headaches, and aches and pains abounded. She used to take Paracetamol and Ibuprofen like they were daily vitamin supplements.

'Was it psychosomatic, or was she really ill?' I questioned. I was confused.

I now know that the constant stream of 'ailments' was used to instil sympathy in me, to ensure that my compassion and care was always there for her; to reinforce the 'rescuer' within me. And that way, my concern and care would be wholly focussed on her, whilst I forgot about myself and neglected my 'Self'.

Her playing the 'victim', the 'helpless child' was effective in securing those 'hooks' deep into me, so that I could *never* leave. After all, if I ever did leave a 'damsel in distress', I would be a despicable person, wouldn't I? This was the very person that deep down I believed I was; and the very person I was determined to annihilate. And loving Yvette was my path of pilgrimage towards that salvation. She was my saviour.

Who needed God to absolve my sins and cleanse my soul, when I could worship at the altar of Yvette? And she was capable of giving me all the love that an ephemeral 'God' couldn't give me. Well, sometimes; if I was 'good'. So I just had to try a little harder.

I learnt through trial and error what pleased her, and what displeased her. I did that because ultimately, her pleasure (or displeasure) would be reflected and projected onto me, and if I was 'good' then I knew that I would be rewarded with the love and attention that I so yearned for.

A junkie needs *regular* 'fixes', and my 'dealer' was the one holding all the crack. Whether I got my 'fix', or not, was up to her; or rather the mood she was in at the time.

One day she returned home from work to the rousing sound of Beethoven's Ninth Symphony. I love the grace and majesty of that symphony, the power of the choir as they sing in harmony with the orchestra in the finale. Her face dropped as she entered the hallway. She didn't talk to me for the rest of the evening. My love for Beethoven was rewarded by the 'silent-treatment'. Of course, it didn't happen again. From that day onwards, I *always* chose music that I knew she liked as she walked through the front door. I knew exactly what time she was due home, and she knew my exact whereabouts at any time. I was hers; completely.

'Surveillance by text' became a part of my life, and if I didn't respond to her inquisitions via text in an 'appropriate' time, then the downward spiral would start. My apparent 'lack of attentiveness' would disappoint her, which would trigger the release of the 'Four horsemen of the apocalypse' who were always there on standby to come to her aid.

The first-horseman was the harbinger of abandonment. An acute fear, either of imaginary or real abandonment ruled her life. Not responding to a text 'on time' or not being available when she 'needed' me opened the doors to 'hell', and the first-horseman was the always there ready to wound me.

He was closely followed by the second-horseman, the harbinger of rage. Her acute impulsivity and lack of emotional regulation caused her to 'act out' and 'vent' her feelings of abandonment in an aggressive way. Shouting, screaming and the 'silent-treatment' were all ways that this horseman could inflict his pain on me.

The third-horseman was the harbinger of rejection: 'If you can't love me in the way I need you to, then I'll find someone else who will!' became a familiar, yet increasingly hurtful weapon to rupture my emotional integrity.

But the fourth-horseman was always the assassinator; he was the one I dreaded the most. I knew that he was the one who could bring me to my knees, and had the power to topple me from that pedestal: He was the harbinger of *devaluation*.

'You're a useless piece of shit and all your past relationships have failed because of your selfishness. You will *always* be on your own, you sad old bastard!'

All of a sudden, in the blink of an eye, my momentary lack of attentiveness meant that I was 'nothing'. I was a shell, devoid of meaning and identity. My life was literally in ruins, because without the ability to love Yvette I was no-one. I didn't know who I was anymore. I just knew that I *had* to get back on that pedestal, at whatever cost to myself.

These changes would take seconds to realise themselves. We could be having a wonderful day, full of joy and happiness. And then a trigger would open the 'gates', and the 'four horsemen' would be on their way.

I was reminded of the film 'The Exorcist', where Father Merrin was tasked with exorcising the demon from within Regan MacNeil. Regan raged at the Father, and threatened to annihilate him. She was able to sense his deepest insecurities, and tried to 'Gas-light' him, to change his perception of reality and undermine the very person he was. She was seductive and tried to disarm him with passion and lust. The end to 'The Exorcist' is a happy one, and Father Merrin was successful in exorcising the demon within Regan. He 'gave himself' to the task, and she was released.

I too was like Father Merrin, a 'rescuer' on my own crusade to 'help' Yvette quell the demons inside her. I thought my love for her was like holy water. I was Jesus on that cross, sacrificing *myself* to chase her demons away forever. I just didn't know at the time that this was one exorcism that wouldn't have a happy ending.

I was spending more and more time with Yvette, and eventually I made the decision to move my home-office to her house. It made sense. Rather than have the long, busy drive to 'work' on the motorway in a morning, I could skip down the stairs to the study instead. I suppose I saw it as a 'half-way-house'; a 'test' of how we could get on before I took the plunge and moved in 'lock, stock and barrel'.

Deep down, our relationship troubled me, but I buried those feelings and ignored them. Denial became a daily practice for me, as subconscious as breathing.

'After all,' I thought, 'this is going to *prove* to her that I do love her and want to be by her side.' The study downstairs doubled as a single bedroom, which my son used to sleep in when he joined us for the weekend. This innocuous room, I later learnt, would become my psychological and physical 'prison' as our dysfunctional relationship careered out of control.

Moving my home-office was a doddle, and I soon settled-in to working, and home-life living with Yvette and her children. We had only been seeing each other five months, and although our frequent 'arguments' troubled me, I reassured myself that this was a good move, and that it would pay dividends. My own house was already on the property market to sell, although since the financial 'meltdown' in two-thousand-and-nine, the market had been in the doldrums. I was confident that it would sell at some point in the future, but secretly I was equally pleased that it wouldn't be in the very near future.

'It would buy me some time,' I thought. Time to make sure that Yvette and I could 'resolve' our issues.

My own children, now teenagers, settled into life with us in our 'new' home. Yvette was initially attentive towards them, and this was reciprocated. When my children came to visit, which was usually every other weekend, we had the slight inconvenience of having to take two cars everywhere to transport the six of us, but I thought this was a minor inconvenience that wasn't an issue. Yvette thought differently.

'Can we look at a new car, so that when we all go out we can all fit in?' she innocently asked one day. 'I'm sure we can afford the repayments, especially if we buy it together and both contribute.'

I knew that taking two cars everywhere annoyed her, and she had made some comments in passing about this before now, but this had been the first time she had mentioned it explicitly. I thought about it. My car was leased through work, and she owned her personally, although it was a little old now with a limited residual value. Buying a newer car, big enough to seat all six of us would have been a considerable expense, and we were already stretched as it was, paying rent on her house, and a mortgage on mine. And also, it was only the occasional weekend we needed such a big car. I was personally happy to persevere with two cars when we needed to take the odd trip together as an extended family. I told her my thoughts about this, and they were met with anger.

'You never listen to my point of view, you controlling, thoughtless bastard!'

I was yet again awash with feelings of anxiety, shame and guilt; feelings that became so familiar to me, and feelings that I learnt to accept and normalise over the year that was to follow. In the end we didn't buy a bigger car; but trust me when I say that she never 'forgave' me for my opinion, and she would always hang onto that 'invalidation', as she saw it. This 'indiscretion' on my part was carefully filed away in her arsenal, to be inflicted against me in the future whenever she needed it.

Around that time, we had similar 'discussions' about my house. Or rather I had 'instructions' from Yvette.

'I think we should rent your house out and get a tenant in. We could do with the extra income.'

Yes, my house was pretty much unused and unoccupied, but I used it occasionally as a 'base' when my children wanted to spend time in the area. They had friends and a life there, that I didn't want to 'close them off' from that just yet. Plus my grumbling concerns about my relationship with Yvette didn't give me the confidence to do that, just yet.

'Well, it's on the market already, and if we get tenants in, it will be more difficult to sell,' I justified. This response was met with the now-familiar silent-treatment.

Yvette *hated* my house. To her, it was a symbol of my independence from her.

I needed to check on my house occasionally, sometimes when returning from working up North, which meant that I would be slightly late back returning to our 'home'. This was met with rage and aggression:

'That fucking house! *I hate it!* Why do you have to check on it? Why? You aren't committed to me at all, you bastard. It's the house, or me!'

My mind was a mess. I was confused and filled with guilt. Was she right? Did I lack commitment to her by not letting go of my 'safety blanket'? No matter how much reassurance I gave her that I loved her, it wasn't enough. My grip on reality was slipping away. We had only been together six months, so was it really 'normal' to move in together so quickly? Was I 'right' to retain my house, just 'in case'? I didn't know anymore. I didn't know what 'truth' and 'reality' were. The only truth I knew was Yvette's 'truth'. And it hurt like hell sometimes.

Yvette's 'tactics' were used with great effect, to try and enmesh me even further. By financially committing to buying a car together, and by letting my house out, it would mean that I would find it even harder to leave her and 'abandon her', as she saw it. But ironically, at the time, leaving her was the very last thing in the world I *ever* wanted to do.

I was being 'Gas-lighted'. Her distorted, perverse version of 'reality' became my version, and I lost the ability to see right or wrong; I lost the ability to think for myself. Through the increasing use of psychological trauma and abuse that I found myself the victim of at her hands, I lost the will to express and retain my own independent thought. I was losing my 'Self', and the constant push-pull dynamics of our relationship were re-traumatising the internal 'wounds' I had carried around since childhood.

But I was in too deep to leave. Cycles of dysfunction punctuated the latter part of that year. I lost count of how many times I had packed up my things and left.

The words: 'Fuck-off! Just leave *now*!' were all too familiar and were now branded on my re-traumatised childhood scars, with the hot-poker of her rage that was so effectively wielded by the 'third-horseman'.

I had a 'system' by November of that year. It had happened so many times; I knew *exactly* how to pack the boot of my car to take all my possessions in one fowl swoop. I dreaded buying additional clothes or other possessions, as they might hinder my 'escape' in the future. But I *always* went back. The Siren was calling for yet another rescue, and I was more than willing to stoke-up my battered, bruised boat to save her, hoping that this time would surely be the last. It never was.

My close friends and family were worried. I think they were starting to question my sanity; they weren't the only ones. My brother was quite categorical:

'Leave her now. Or she'll *destroy* you!'

Destroy me? How? I was in so deep that I truly believed the only thing that *would* destroy me would be if I left her. How could I walk away from my 'Soul-mate', the true love of my life? She was my salvation. I couldn't function without her. I didn't want to live without her. But my brother was right. And she almost did destroy me. And I just sat there and took it.

December arrived, and I wasn't even sure if we would be spending Christmas together that year, our 'first' Christmas together. In early December it looked likely, but in mid-December I had been rejected, devalued and pushed-away once more. But we *did* spend

Christmas together in the end; just by the 'skin of our teeth'. But just like any other plans we had together, it was unpredictable and uncertain whether they would actually 'happen' or not, up until the eleventh-hour.

The 'push-pull' cycle of destruction was starting to take its toll on me. My work was suffering, as were my relationships with close friends and family.

The 'Black Widow' had almost completed her psychological web of restraint, and the thought of escape was now incomprehensible to me.

Like the spider said to the fly:

'All the better to ensnare you with my dear... all the better to ensnare you with...'

Chapter 9

Thankfully, the first few months of the New Year were relatively quiet. Our cycles of dysfunction seemed to get less frequent, and I had renewed confidence that I would indeed be able to 'commit' to Yvette completely. Because by that stage, I believed that our dysfunction was my entire fault, wasn't it? I had accepted the 'blame', fairly and squarely; I now carried the full weight of our relationship on my shoulders.

I just wasn't aware at the time of all the things I needed to dishevel myself of, in order to carry that weighty burden. I had lost my self-esteem, my self-confidence and my grip on reality. I was losing my friends, my family and my children. But I believed it was a price worth paying when I was firmly on that pedestal, surveying the wondrous altar of Yvette that I could worship at.

Unfortunately, my false optimism at the time would be short-lived, because this was going to turn out to be the worst year of my life.

I decided in the New Year to eventually get a tenant in my house. After all, we were making plans for the future. We had a family holiday to Tenerife booked at Easter-time, and my denial of our problems was almost complete. The 'Gas-lighting' was working reinforced, of course, by frequent, but unpredictable abuse and devaluation.

It was quite easy to find a tenant for my house, and they arranged to move in at the end of February. I had done it! I had finally managed to 'commit' to the woman I loved with every breath of my body. I had let go, and it felt good. I was busy making plans to put my household possessions in storage, arranging removals and organising the letting. This pleased Yvette no end. I was her 'hero' again, and I believed that I *would* save her from the abyss after all.

The 'dysfunctional dance' that we had been engaged in seemed to cease for a while. Maybe the merry-go-round had finally come to a stop? I relaxed, and for the first time in a long time I didn't feel anxious about the present or the future.

The move went well, and we had an amazing time in Tenerife as a family at Easter-time. At that time we had been living together 'properly' for a couple of months, and my tenant and her family had settled in well.

'Everything was going to be great,' I reassured myself. All my previous fears had been for nothing. And the future looked rosy. Unfortunately all that was to change when we returned from Tenerife in April...

Juggling two young families with ex's posed its challenges. My ex-wife and I had been divorced for a number of years, and we had a 'working' relationship. We were far from close, but we both had the best interests of our children at heart, and we communicated primarily using email. It worked. Just.

Yvette's relationship with her second ex-husband, Liam was very different. For the past year she had told me of the 'awful abuse' that she had endured at his hands, about how he was controlling and manipulative, even towards their young children. He was a demon, and she needed me to 'side' with her against him.

I met Liam a number of times, a jovial guy who always smiled and said 'Hello,' when he either picked up the children from Yvette's, or dropped them off. I had been witness to some pretty heated altercations between them on the doorstep over the last year. Thinking back, they were usually one-sided, and they usually entailed Yvette screaming and raging at him on her doorstep, in front of their young children. At that time they had been separated for around a year, so I just 'chalked it up' to an acrimonious divorce, and overlooked it. But something was wrong; very wrong.

'Why don't you believe me about Liam?' she quizzed me one day.

'What do you mean?' I replied. 'I've only met him a handful of times, and we've only exchanged pleasantries. I don't know him at all. But if you say what went on did go on, then I believe you.'

I thought that would be the end of it. The *truth* was that I didn't know Liam, and he had always been pleasant. I had no reason to demonise him myself.

She wouldn't let it drop.

'No, you *always* take his side, and I *never* feel supported by you!' she went on.

My feelings of anxiety were starting to rise again.

'Yvette, I *don't know* Liam, and I'm not going to form an opinion about someone I don't know!'

Why should I demonise a man I didn't even know? Why should I join her in her crusade of hate and tyranny towards him? I stood my ground, but it cost me. The punishment was a day of the dreaded silent-treatment.

Children aside, Yvette and I were lucky that we had weekends together without any parental responsibilities, when all our children were with our respective ex's. We spent that time in a variety of ways. We loved the theatre, the cinema, and we often just spent the weekend in bed devouring each other. It was 'our' time and we loved it.

Because she had to do some residential on-call at the hospital she presently worked at, some of our weekends were spent in a budget hotel not too far from her hospital, so that she could attend to sick patients when she needed to. If she had no pressing duties to attend to, we were also free to wander around the local town. In my mind, it didn't matter where we were; as long as we were together.

She found separation extremely difficult, and on the occasions where I hadn't been able to accompany her on her on-call weekend duties, it made for a stormy time. And I was intent on doing *anything* I could to reduce those times, especially now that we were living together.

When we returned from Tenerife, there was an email in my inbox from my ex-wife. She informed me that she had to change her plans because of work, and would I mind swapping a weekend with her, so that I would be with our children a weekend earlier than was planned in the schedule. I consulted our schedule. That weekend was one of the weekends that Yvette was residential on-call at the hospital. I wanted to see my children, and thought of a way I could please everyone, so I agreed with my ex-wife that this change would be fine. But I was also committed to spending time with Yvette that weekend, even if it meant me and my children staying at home, and paying daily visits to her in the hospital, or meeting up in the local town.

I informed Yvette of this change to our schedule. And all hell broke loose.

'What am I going to do without you!?' she shouted. 'You *always* choose your fucking kids over me!'

I tried in vain to calm her, to reassure her that I would visit her with the children in the day, and that we would see plenty of each other that weekend. To no avail. The shouting escalated, the abuse much more profane, and the devaluation was crippling. I was at breaking point. What could I do? I wanted to run, but I had nowhere to run to, now that my house was let-out.

I sobbed. I fell to the floor and sobbed. I *had* to get out. I grabbed my car keys, and dashed for the door. I floored the accelerator in a bid to escape the pain, and switched my mobile off. I knew what was coming next. And I literally couldn't take any more of it.

Where should I go? What was I meant to do? Had I been unfair to Yvette? Should I have declined the request from my ex-wife? My mind was filled with questions and self-doubt, and my soul was filled with shame and guilt, but it had never felt this bad before. I had left her yet again. I had deserted her in a way I promised myself that I would *never* do again. I had abandoned her yet again, and for that I deserved punishing.

I wanted to die. I fantasised about hitting a brick wall with my car, seatbelt unbuckled, to stop the pain.

I found myself on a nearby industrial estate, parked up in the pitch black. And all that could probably be heard for miles around me were my cries of pain. I sobbed, until I could sob no more. I felt alone, isolated. Who could I turn to? Where could I go? After a couple of hours I had calmed myself, and decided to return. It was the only place I could go; back into the abyss.

I pulled up in front of the house to find a Police car parked there. With trepidation, I slowly turned the key in the lock and wished I could be invisible. All I wanted was for Yvette to love me; to cherish me. Had I failed in that endeavour? Had I failed in the same way I had done in trying to make my mother love me? I felt worthless, and my mind raced as I climbed the stairs.

On reaching the lounge, there was a Police officer sat there consoling Yvette.

'Where have you been!' she exclaimed. 'I had to call the Police because you hadn't come back. I've been worried sick about you!'

In front of the Police officer, she tried desperately to conceal her anger, and feigned concern instead. There she was; the source of my pain. And I *wanted* concern from her, not anger. I mumbled to the Police officer that I had gone for a drive, and that I can't seem to 'please anyone'. I started sobbing again.

'Do you have a good relationship with your ex and your children?' he asked.

'Yes,' I replied.

'Listen,' he continued, 'try not to be so hard on yourself? I'm sure your children think the world of you, and you have a lovely, supportive partner here to help you,' gesturing at Yvette. I felt nauseous and managed to swallow a mouthful of sick that was now stuck in my oesophagus.

I wanted to cry out: 'Lovely, supportive partner! NO! She's the one who's abusing me! SHE'S the one who is causing me all this pain!'

But I didn't. I kept my silence.

He pulled himself off the sofa and reassured both myself and a distraught Yvette that everything was going to be fine. She saw him to the front door, and then I heard her footsteps come back towards the lounge, like distant cracks of thunder.

'Please hold me!?' I thought. 'PLEASE hold me and tell me that everything is going to be OK?' I was lost, and all I wanted was for Yvette to hold me and comfort me. I was a little lost child, awash in my anguish. And I *needed* her; either her or my mother.

Once the Police officer was safely dispatched, she turned on me like a woman possessed.

'Don't you EVER do that again, you worthless cunt!' she screamed at the top of her voice. 'You KNOW that's one thing I can't cope with, and next time you do it you are OUT!'

No comforting; no sympathy. Just pain.

'Now fuck-off to the spare room you useless piece of shit!'

With that, her deliberate footsteps directed towards our bedroom were my cue to take my position. I retreated to a spare bedroom that was my new prison cell, and I cried myself to sleep.

If I *was* ever to leave again, I had to make sure it was for the last time...

Chapter 10

I awoke after a restless slumber. My torture wasn't over when I was relegated to the spare room the evening before. Yvette had been texting abuse to me from upstairs throughout the night, and my mobile was full of messages filled with hate.

I _had_ to get out. My survival depended on it. But how? I felt powerless and weak against this immovable force.

I couldn't really read her text messages, because they hurt so much. I didn't realise that I could be devalued any further, but I could. She _always_ found a way.

One of the text messages that caught my eye told me that she deserved someone far 'better' than me, and that she would be going back on findyourmatch.com to find them. This was a familiar pattern when we spiralled into our dysfunctional dance. I lost count of the number of times she had reactivated her profile on the website in the last year when we fought. After all, if she couldn't get the attention and adulation from me when she pushed me away and I 'abandoned' her, she could find it elsewhere.

She was a desperately attractive woman, and didn't find it hard to attract male attention. Going back on findyourmatch.com fed her narcissism, and also gave her a few options to try and 'triangulate' if thing's weren't going to work out with me. The thought of her flirting with other men online filled me with anger and self-pity. How could she be so cruel? How could she do this?

The last few weeks had been mentally gruelling, and I was starting to 'catch fleas'. I found myself doing things that were _completely_ out of character for me, in a desperate attempt to salvage the relationship. One of those things was accessing her email, and findyourmatch.com accounts. Her password was easy to guess, and it gave me an insight into what she was doing.

I spent the day in a fervour of activity, and there were two things on my mind. The first was to engineer a way *out* of here, and the second was to find out what was going on in that head of hers. I had so many questions, but so few answers.

Getting out. It wouldn't be easy, and I would have to make my plans carefully, and undetected in order that I didn't get 'hoovered' back in.

I was due to go back to my house imminently and carry out a landlord-check, so I hastily arranged an appointment with my tenant for later that week. I knew what I needed to do: ask my tenant to vacate my house. She hadn't been in the house three-months yet, but I needed to get back to safety.

I saw my tenant later that week, and I made my proposal of a month's rent 'in hand' if she would vacate early. She said that she would need to think about it, which gave me a shaft of hope to cling onto. Meanwhile, I secured a storage unit not too far from my house, so when the time came I could remove all my possessions to the unit. I planned to disappear, literally. I also asked a friend to help me with the removals, and we agreed we would set a date when I had heard from my tenant, or alternatively if I had no other option but to find other accommodation to move into.

Thankfully, it didn't take too long for my tenant to get back to me. A couple of days later, she phoned to say that she would be happy to leave in about three-weeks time. That gave me three-weeks of planning to leave *for good*. It would be 'tight', and probably the hardest three-weeks of my life, but I *had* to do it for my sanity. Yvette and I weren't really talking too much at that time, and I had accepted my prison cell for the time being, which gave me plenty of time to covertly make my escape plans.

Whilst I was 'busy' and distant, she made it quite clear to me that she planned to date other people; unless I reengaged with her, of course. I was desperate to know what was going on, so I hacked her email accounts and began reading…

Her flirtations on findyourmatch.com were sickening. She used exactly the 'same lines' with others that she had used with me over a year ago. I found out who she was communicating with, and when they planned to meet. The scale of her flirtation was astounding, her setting-up several dates in a single day. She was obviously *desperate* to find someone else. But why? Hadn't I been good enough for her? The wave of toxic guilt and shame returned.

In my desperation, in the depths of my solitude all alone in the spare room, I perversely hoped that she would reach out to me, and love me. I felt scared and alone.

Then it happened, on my second night in 'solitary'. A knock at the door. It was Yvette. She was seductive, warm, and soft - and wanted me. I succumbed to her physicality, to her alluring sexuality and we made-love, repeatedly, on the floor. My head was spinning. I had been drawn back in. And I *hated* myself for it. *Yet again* she was willing to put me back on that pedestal, and yet again I was willing to take my place. But what would I do about the plans I was making to escape? Should I stop them?

Whilst reading her emails a few days later, I noticed a few emails from her ex-husband, Liam. I needed answers, and I needed them quickly. I was becoming increasingly confused and I felt like I was losing touch with reality. I decided that I would email Liam, and ask him if he wouldn't mind meeting up for a chat. Surprisingly, he readily agreed.

Apart from being Yvette's ex-husband, Liam was also a psychologist. Surely *he* would have some answers for me, to help explain her bizarre behaviour. We agreed that I would go around and see him on one of the nights that Yvette was working on-call at the hospital. Tentatively, I knocked on the door and waited. Liam was welcoming, and invited me to come in. We spent the next couple of hours deep in conversation.

'Why is Yvette like this?' I asked.

'Well,' he said, 'I believe she has a condition called Borderline Personality Disorder.'

I'd never heard of Borderline Personality Disorder, or 'BPD'. What was it? And how could it go towards explaining Yvette's extreme behaviour? I was committed to learning more about the condition; deep down I was committed to 'saving' Yvette from it. Although I didn't know it at the time, those three words were going to change my life forever.

I went on to tell Liam, 'I think I want to leave, but I'm not sure I do, or how?'

'You're probably going to find it very difficult,' he replied, 'because you're probably suffering from Stockholm's Syndrome.'

What? I had a condition? Was there something wrong with *me*? I was confused when I left Liam that night, probably more confused than before I had arrived on his doorstep. And it would take me many months to find the answers that I needed.

It didn't take long for my mind to be made up one way or the other about my relationship with Yvette though. Or so I thought at the time.

One night a few days later, she was yet again residential on-call at her hospital. She went into free-fall. The abuse and devaluation in her texts knew no bounds, and I refused to answer her calls.

In the end, she threatened suicide. She talked about connecting a hose-pipe to the exhaust-pipe of her car, and suffocating herself. I was distraught. What should I do? Who should I call? My first thought was to contact Liam. By then I had his mobile number, and I sent him a text to relay to him what was happening.

'Oh, don't worry,' he replied, 'She's threatened it B4 & never goes thru with it. I would just call the police to let them know.'

I didn't want to call the Police, in case I got Yvette into trouble, so I chose to call her hospital instead. I spoke to the Sister on the ward, and asked her to check on Yvette as soon as she possibly could. A few minutes later I received a threatening text from Yvette:

'Don't U DARE involve my hospital in this, U CUNT!!!!'

I was scared; scared for myself. She followed it up with another threat: 'If U don't leave my house by 8 2morrow morning, I will come back and smash 2 bits everything that U have left!!!'

87

My mind was made up. I must leave *now*! By that point, I had the keys to the storage unit near my house, and I quickly bundled as many of my possessions as I could into the car. I knew it was going to take a few loads to get my stuff out, so I worked quickly and managed to drop one load off that evening, before the storage facility closed. I returned to my prison cell that evening, hopefully for the last time I thought.

Early in the morning I managed to get another load up safely to the unit, which left one more trip for the remaining small items. There were also some heavier, bulkier items that I couldn't fit in my car, like the TV and sound-system, but I committed to leaving those and to 'write them off'. After all, the chances of me returning for them later and them still being in one piece seemed slight.

Eventually I managed to drive away with the final load, safe in the knowledge that it was probably my remaining possessions that would be physically damaged, rather than me. I thought I was free. But then again, my thoughts had been deceiving and 'twisted' before...

I had no-where to go, and my life was in tatters. What should I do? Where *should* I go? I had around five days to wait until my tenant vacated my house. After I deposited the last load of my possessions in the storage unit, I needed somewhere to go. But where?

I decided to check-in to a budget hotel near my house, and just wait there to get back in. I didn't know what I was going to do in that time. I couldn't work, so I called in sick. My mind and spirit felt completely 'broken'.

The next few days were hell. I felt shell-shocked and emotionally numb. Why did I *still* miss her and want her, I thought, especially after everything she's done to me?

I couldn't function. My life stopped, in a way that I had never experienced before. I was grasping at straws; anything to stop the pain that I was feeling. What was Borderline Personality Disorder? I thought. What was this 'condition' that appeared to have ravaged my life beyond all recognition? I spent the next few days deep in research. I learnt about the condition, what could cause it, it's 'symptoms' and how to treat it. I must admit, at that time it wasn't making complete sense. How could this condition cause so much damage? How could one person's actions have such a massive impact on others?

I scanned the 'DSM-IV-TR' diagnostic criteria for BPD on the internet. Yvette had the vast majority of them, and only five out of nine were needed to 'confirm' a diagnosis. Yes, I could see that all the signs and symptoms were there, but why?

I read about the possible causes of BPD, including a neglectful, traumatic childhood. Yes, Yvette had experienced a particularly traumatic childhood at the hands of her abusive mother. Her father had died when she was very young, and her mother used to physically beat her and abandon her before sending her, in her formative years, to live with distant family relatives, who also physically abused her. She had had a tough life, poor thing. Although I hadn't had a conversation with Yvette about BPD, I was pretty sure that she was undiagnosed, or even in denial about the condition. And it was at that point I felt pity for her. I felt sorry for her. And I felt, yet again, that I wanted to help her and 'rescue' her.

I was scared, very scared. I wasn't sleeping. I wasn't living; I just existed. And I became obsessed with knowing everything I could about BPD. I delved deeper and deeper into the condition that I 'blamed' for my pain. I blamed Yvette. I vilified her, but couldn't find it within myself to hate her or feel angry towards her. Why? Why did I want to go back to her? Why did I hate *myself* so much? I was tortured with questions that I didn't have the answers to.

Eventually, the day came to take possession of my house again. But it wasn't a happy day; it wasn't 'joyous'. Far from it. I was in the depths of despair. I felt a failure, again. I hadn't *made* her love me. I blamed her BPD for my predicament, yet simultaneously blamed myself for 'not loving her enough'. I wanted her back, and at that time I thought I would do *anything* to do it. Reality was slipping away, and I lost complete touch with my 'Self'.

My inner child came back to haunt me, and I dissociated from life. I felt like I had *lost* my life, and that I had *lost* my 'Self'. Even though she had hurt me more than anyone had done before in my adult life, I *needed* her back. And it was that dissociation which ravaged my life for the next few weeks.

Chapter 11

The famous French philosopher Henri Bergson once said:

'Life does not proceed by the association and addition of elements, but by dissociation and division.'

But what is dissociation, and why is it relevant to my story? The 'American Psychiatric Association' has defined dissociation as 'the disruption of the usually integrated functions of consciousness, memory, identity, or perception of the environment.'

Dissociation is something every one of us uses from time-to-time. It's how we 'suspend belief' and 'escape from reality'.

Have you ever taken a car journey and wondered how you got where you were going without conscious thought? Time just seems to 'evaporate'. The chances are you were dissociating, or 'daydreaming'.

An appreciation of music requires some level of dissociation. To 'truly' immerse oneself in music, of whatever kind requires you to suspend rationality and to 'believe' that what you are experiencing is more than just other human beings playing notes on musical instruments.

Music had always been a great passion of mine, right from the very time I could first remember hearing ABBA play on the radio when I was six years-old. I quickly 'learned' to immerse myself in music, and I became well 'practised' at dissociation in doing that. I just adored music, and I surrounded myself with it. But at the same time as a developing child, I had to learn to dissociate to deal with something far more sinister; the systematic abuse of my 'Self' by my Mother...

A small child is powerless to resist their primary caregiver. I can still remember and 'feel' the twisted knot in my stomach that appeared when I knew my mother was going to strike me. I pushed it down, deep down within me to prevent myself feeling pain and anger. Not just physical pain, but psychological pain. I *couldn't* be angry towards my mother. I loved her. So I didn't *allow* myself to feel anger when she hit me.

In effect, I 'split' and divided my emotions when she abused me. I buried my anger and pain deep down, and promised myself that I wouldn't feel those things towards her; that I wouldn't feel those feelings *ever*. When she hit me I dissociated. I 'took myself off' somewhere else and rejected the reality of the abuse she was perpetrating. That was the only way I could enable myself to carry on loving her.

Dissociation from abuse is well documented. Abuse forms 'scars' within 'core-damaged' adult-children, scars that impact on how that person develops emotionally. Healthy children become 'lost children', as described by the psychologist Alice Miller. They have 'hidden' scars and repressed anger, unseen to the naked eye, but felt subconsciously every single day in their adult lives. Dissociation becomes a way of life. And it was that dissociation that I continued to practise so well in my abusive relationship with Yvette.

Dissociation 'allows' soldiers to kill others at point-blank-range, people that they don't know, and 'allows' them to commit the most mortal 'sin' against mankind without feeling remorse; well, that's before Post Traumatic Stress Disorder (PTSD) kicks in. And some 'damaged' adult-children do indeed become soldiers who kill, in order to carry on dissociating.

But some 'damaged' children also become psychopaths, rapists, murderers and thieves who display no 'remorse' for their crimes, because they dissociate. To them, what they perpetrate aren't 'crimes'; their acts are a means of survival. And the moral-relativism of 'right vs. wrong' is something that these monsters can't appreciate and comprehend. To themselves, they are 'god'; untouchable.

However, some of these 'damaged' children subconsciously choose to become carers and caretakers. Their 'calling' to others is needed to feed their deep-seated narcissism. In 'helping' others and 'giving themselves' to others, they can make themselves 'believe' that they are 'good' people after all; that their mothers were 'wrong' for telling them that they were worthless and vile, a psychological self-defence, or protective response to the physical and emotional abuse that they suffered.

It's no surprise then that the caring professions 'called' both myself and Yvette. These professions were 'salvations' from our demonic selves. And it was no 'accident' that Yvette became a doctor.

The term 'Borderline Personality Disorder' was initially coined because it was thought that these people were lying on the 'borderline' between psychosis and neurosis. It's not important to dwell on this too much further, except to say that Yvette lived her life in a complete disarray of dissociation, completely immersed in it in order to deal with her childhood 'scars'. We were both 'damaged' in different ways, and responded to our scars in different ways.

People who dissociate have difficulty in appreciating reality. They don't actually know what reality is, apart from what the constant pain of their internal scars tell them it is. People who dissociate may believe that they are indeed 'good' people, when societal morality could conversely see them as 'bad'. They delude themselves into constructing a reality that may be very different from the actual 'truth', in order to survive.

Yvette lived with a constant fear of imaginary or actual abandonment. Her 'reality' was that whomever she loved would eventually abandon her, in the same way that her mother did when she was a child. To cope with these crippling fears, she 'split' herself into two; she had a 'fractured self'. Rather then allowing herself to 'feel' those crippling feelings, those irrational fears of abandonment, and express them healthily she tried to bury them within her inner child, and lock them away.

Her primary 'tool' to help her achieve that end was control; total control of her environment, and total control of the people around her. In our relationship, I became her primary caregiver. I became the person who loved her. And she needed to control me *completely*. By controlling me, dictating what I did, whom I saw and even what I thought and felt, she deluded herself into thinking that she had the ability to stave off her perpetual fear of abandonment. Whilst we were living together, and even before then, predictability became imperative for her to survive.

Whilst I was with Yvette, seeing my friends without her became difficult. Spending time alone, without her, became impossible. Caring for my own children in her absence was met with rage and abuse; because all these things that I 'did' re-traumatised her childhood scars, and reinforced the dualistic reality within her. And the duality was that she *couldn't* control me, and that I *would* eventually abandon her. And she couldn't cope with this. So as a defence mechanism, she 'acted out', threw abuse towards me and pushed me away, before I could leave *her*. It was the only way she knew how to regain 'control' of the skewed, distorted world around her.

Yvette was clingy and needy right from the very start of our relationship. She tried very hard to 'hide' this at first, but she drew me in with her tales of woe. And at the start I put it down to irrational 'jealousy'. Her clinginess was actually slightly endearing, appealing as it did to my own narcissistic ego. Maybe she was just a little insecure? Maybe she needed constant reassurance that I did indeed love her? And of course, I was more than happy to oblige as a narcissistic co-dependent myself.

But the insatiable need of a Borderline for reassurance and attention can *never* be satisfied. They're called 'Emotional Vampires' for a good reason. No matter how hard I tried whilst we were together, no matter how much attention and reassurance I gave her, it was never enough. And I was *forever* at risk of falling from that pedestal that I loved so much.

In response to her irrational fears about abandonment and engulfment, she abused me emotionally whilst we were together. She 'vented' and 'acted out', pushed me away then reeled me back in time and time again; because she *needed* me. The type of 'push-pull' love that we experienced in our relationship exactly mirrored her experiences in loving her mother when she was a child. Our relational dynamics felt 'natural' to her. She was unable to love without feeling the pain that had always been associated with that. She was a 'core-damaged' adult-child in this world, just like I was.

The feelings I felt when Yvette abused me were feelings I knew all too well from my childhood. Our dysfunction felt natural to me too; to feel pain with love was something I too was used to feeling. Because it was exactly what *I* had felt in trying to love my mother.

In essence, we were both replaying our relationships with our primary caregivers when we were children; with our mothers. And we were both intent on rewriting history. She was intent on receiving from me the unconditional love that she failed to receive from her mother when she was a child, and I was intent on 'making' her love me in a way that I had failed to in my relationship with my own mother. The thing is, even though my mother abused me, I still loved her. And I had exactly the same feelings towards Yvette, even after everything that had happened.

'Stockholm's Syndrome' is a condition of the mind brought about by enduring abuse. It takes its name from a bank robbery in Stockholm in nineteen-seventy-three, where bank employees were violently held hostage by a gang within the bank for a number of days. Bizarrely, after the siege was over and the hostages were freed, some of them defended the actions of the gang, some even going so far as to raise funds to have them freed. 'Capture-bonding' is key to this concept, where abuser and victim become emotionally enmeshed. And holding people hostage, emotionally, is the result.

Although I didn't know it at the time, in those desperate weeks after I returned to my own house, I was suffering from Stockholm's Syndrome. I was totally and utterly 'in love' and obsessed with my captor. Who in this case was Yvette. I needed to return to her. I needed to love her.

When people who are enmeshed in 'capture bonding' experience the loss of their captor, they experience desperation. This explains why I reacted the way I did when I left my own mother to go to University all those years ago. I was distraught and overcome with despair at the time. I remember many times sobbing down the phone to my mother, telling her that I 'just wanted to come home!' At many points in that first term when I started my course, I wanted to 'jack it all in' and go home; go home to my abuser.

Exactly the same applied in my relationship with Yvette. I wanted, more than anything in the world, to return to her. I literally couldn't live without her. I was completely preoccupied with thoughts of her.

Obviously, at that particular time in my story I was completely unaware (or in denial) of my Stockholm's Syndrome – otherwise I would *never* have done what I did next...

Chapter 12

Following my return to my house in late-May, my life as I had known it before had literally disappeared.

I became obsessed with learning about BPD, and how it could be 'cured'. Because deep down, I wanted to cure Yvette of this ravaging 'disease'. I stopped working, completely. I stopped eating, and lost almost a stone in weight. My crutches became alcohol and nicotine, neither of which filled the painful void within me.

In desperation, I went to see my GP, who prescribed me Fluoxitine and recommended counselling. I took the tablets for around a week, and never followed up on counselling. After all, I didn't want either of those; I didn't want my pain to go away. All I wanted was Yvette back, and I felt I would do anything to do that.

I was trying to go 'cold turkey', and disengage from the most addictive drug I had ever experienced: My love for Yvette. She was my 'dealer' and she was the holder of my happiness, or so I believed. But I knew my 'dealer' was still there, and at the time I always thought she would be, in my very consciousness.

I ached for her to reach out to me, to need me. And then it happened. A call came one Wednesday night, just after her birthday. I answered, and immediately got the 'fix' I had so badly needed. It was Yvette. She was distraught, sobbing down the phone. I immediately jumped into the car and went back to my nemesis, yet again.

I almost broke the front door down; I was so desperate to see her. I held her so tightly, that at one point I thought I would crush her frail body, which like my own had lost many of its curves that were there when we last embraced.

'Come back to me, please!?' she screamed. 'Yes, yes, yes!' I replied.

That night we made-love as if there was no tomorrow, totally immersing ourselves in one-another. I was back. And there was no place on this earth that I would have preferred to have been.

In the morning she told me about how she had met someone else a few weeks ago. They met on findyourmatch.com, and it was one of the people with whom she had been flirting with when I accessed her account just before I moved out in May. She told me in great detail about how they had met, where they had been, and how they had made-love on their second date. I seethed with jealously. But I was with her now. And that was all that mattered.

She went on to tell me about how he 'wasn't her type after all,' how he was always busy and was never there for her. 'But I was there for her,' I thought, and I would *always* be there for her.

We both wanted to try again, and this time we would 'make it right'. We were both committed to that. I suggested that we go to 'couples counselling' again, to try and help us communicate. I thought at the time that was the key to stopping our 'dysfunctional dance'. I obviously didn't fully understand BPD when I suggested that at the time. We had tried joint-counselling briefly before I had moved out, but at the time it didn't work. I remember feeling persecuted in the two brief sessions we had, as if Yvette was trying to turn the counsellor against me, to 'gang up' on me with her. I remember feeling scared of Yvette in those sessions, and scared of what she would say to me after they had finished.

The next couple of weeks were filled with joy and passion. We were back, and at the time it felt like it was better than it had ever been before. We talked about the future, even telling friends that we wanted to get married the following year. I moved some of my things back from my house, and we resumed living together as a couple. This time it *would* be right, I told myself. She appeared committed to making it work and couples-counselling seemed better than before. 'Maybe it would help this time?' I thought.

Unbeknown to Yvette, I was still in touch with her ex-husband, Liam. I felt a little bad about this, like I was 'cheating' on her in a way, but he had been good to me and knew my situation. He had also given me the 'key', so I thought, to helping Yvette, the knowledge I now had about BPD and a possible way I could help her.

My 'rescuing' tendencies were now in full-swing, and I was committed to 'saving' her. When I told Liam via email of my plans to make it work this time, he seemed cautious.

'Be careful,' he replied, 'we tried couples-counselling and everything else that we could when we had exactly the same problems. In the end, I *had* to leave Yvette when she came at me with a knife.'

It felt like my heart had stopped for a second. A knife! At first, I was in denial, yet again. Surely he's making it up? I knew their split was acrimonious, and Yvette had told me lots of things about him, but a *knife*? Surely not!

I couldn't get this thought out of my mind in the next few days. But for the first time in over a year, I started 'listening' to myself. I chose not to deny, and instead to acknowledge my feelings. I knew Liam was right. I knew, deep down, that this beautiful creature whom I believed I loved with all of my heart and soul could be capable of doing this.

So why was I still there? Why was I continuing to put myself in danger? Although our 'fights' had never become physical so far, I knew deep down that there was potential for them to.

I felt like I had to share my knowledge of BPD with Yvette at some point, to help her realise what the problem was, and to ultimately help her to seek therapy. I continued to carry her concerns around on my shoulders, continued to live for 'her' rather than myself. And I naively thought that 'sharing' my knowledge about BPD would enable me to drop this increasingly-weighty load, and that it would be the key to our future happiness. All I needed to do now was to choose an appropriate time to share this with her. And I didn't have to wait very long...

Yvette couldn't take any form of personal criticism, from *anyone*. In her eyes, she had to be perfect. She had to be 'right' all of the time. She saw every difference between us, every difference of opinion, as an attack on her 'Self'. Agreeing to disagree was impossible for her.

One Sunday morning we got into a discussion about a legal case that was in the paper that week. We had a difference of opinion, and I could tell she was 'stung'; she was triggered and that tsunami of emotion was on its way again. Because we had a disagreement, about something that wasn't directly or even indirectly relevant to our life together, I fell off my pedestal yet again. No longer her knight in shining amour, I was now the devil incarnate. She spiralled out of control.

'Your opinion is shit! All your opinions are! That's all you are, a useless cunt! I don't want you. I need someone who shares the same opinions as me!!'

In the blink of an eye I was being devalued as quickly as I had been idolised an hour before, but now I thought I knew why. Her acute fear of abandonment had kick-in yet again, because I was no longer her 'hero'. In the way she *perceived* reality, I would no longer be able to 'save' her because my 'colour' had changed in a heartbeat. I was no longer 'white'; I was 'black', as black as the abyss itself. She was completely unable to appreciate shades of 'grey' within either herself, or other people she loved, and 'splitting' between good/bad or white/black was the only way she could operate emotionally. Yvette was a three year-old girl inside a grown woman's body, and her 'tantrums' were how her fractured, inner child expressed their feelings and emotions.

All of her internal pain and anguish was being projected onto me, and by 'venting' in that way she was determined to make me the part of herself she wanted to rid herself of so desperately. By projecting it onto me, she had the perfect way to deflect these feelings; feelings of inadequacy and self-loathing that she had carried around since childhood.

Now was my time, I thought. Now would be the time to tell her.

'Yvette, I think you have a condition called Borderline Personality Disorder, or BPD.'

She stopped mid-sentence. Her mouth fell open and her eyes widened. It felt like an eternity, sat there, waiting for a reaction. In the couple of seconds I was waiting, I hoped for some questions from her, a rational response; I hoped she would calm down and almost be 'shocked' out of her rage. What came next, I would never have predicted:

'Fuck-off you cunt! Get out of my life forever, you piece of shit! Leave! Just fuck-off and leave NOW!'

I thought for a second that she was going to hit me. Deep down, I actually *wanted* her to hit me, in the same way that my own mother used to strike me as a child. Instead, she leaped off the bed, went over to the wardrobe and started throwing my own clothes at me, enraged, like a wild animal. I went over to touch her, hold her, to console her. She pushed me away violently, and then ran down the stairs.

I heard the front door slam behind her, and then her car accelerate away from the house. She was gone. Until the next time. Because unfortunately the orchestra was still playing, and our dysfunctional dance was *far* from over.

Chapter 13

My mobile rang a few minutes later. It was Yvette.

'I want you out NOW, you cunt!' she shouted down the phone. 'I'm at a friend's house, and if you're not gone when I come back home in ten minutes, I'm calling the Police!'

Panic took over me. Was she bluffing? Or did she mean it? I didn't know. I felt like I didn't know this woman whom I believed I loved so dearly. She was someone else now. She was 'acting out' the part of her that I know she loathed and hated; the part of her that she was projecting onto me and wanted *me* to become. When this damaged inner-child 'came out' her impulsivity knew no bounds. She was completely unable to regulate her emotions. What she felt, she felt justified in expressing whether that was good, or bad, there and then without temperament. There was no 'filter', no ability to rationalise and reason with her 'Self'; because her identity was fractured and 'broken'.

When she felt good about life and about me, then I could do no wrong. I was 'perfect' in her eyes. But no-one really is perfect, and we all have 'faults'. However, 'faults' and ambiguity don't exist in a Borderline's psyche. Black and white thinking and 'splitting' is all they have the emotional capacity to deal with. Conversely, if she felt bad about life, then I was the natural perpetrator of that negativity. And she would make me pay for it, one way or another; devaluation was always her 'trump card'.

I decided to go. I didn't want to call her bluff. I didn't trust her. The worst thing was I didn't trust myself. I had been 'Gas-lighted' for so long, and neither knew right from wrong, nor good from bad. My perception of reality had been twisted out of all comprehension. All I knew was that I couldn't live without her.

I ran. That adrenaline rush associated with 'fight or flight' flooded my system. I couldn't 'fight' even if I had wanted to, even if she had been there to 'fight' with; my childhood conditioning would have made that impossible anyway. So I had to run. I threw what I needed into a cheap supermarket plastic bag, and ran.

I got back to my house and broke down, yet again. I committed to myself at that point that I *had* to get out of this relationship. I couldn't reason with Yvette. It was impossible. But I doubted myself. I doubted my thoughts; doubted my feelings. The texts started. Abuse, denigration and devaluation.

'I'm going 2 find myself sumone who is worthy of my love! You cunt!'

The next few texts appeared as if she was talking to a lover, someone whom she may have been in touch with:

'Can't wait 2 C U day after 2morrow! X' 'Yes, I'm all urs 2. At least I will B then ;-) X'

I'm not sure if these were 'genuine' or not, but it didn't matter; they hurt exactly the same. That familiar feeling in my stomach returned, the feeling that I experienced when my mother was about to strike me.

The texts were relentless, and the 'ping' of a new text arriving from her filled me with dread. I couldn't bear to switch off my mobile. It was my only connection with the woman whom I *still* adored. I eventually fell asleep that night, if sleep was what you could call it.

I awoke the next morning, and knew what I needed to do. There were too many of my possessions at

Yvette's house to squeeze into the boot of my car, so I decided to hire a van, and was committed to returning to the house as soon as I possibly could to collect *all* of my things. At least I *thought* I was committed. My childhood scars were telling me something else...

I had arranged to see my own children that day. My daughter wanted to go shopping in the local town, and we planned to have lunch afterwards. I dragged the 'shell' of myself that I had now become around the shopping centre, my head spinning with confusion, and my soul filled with pain. I had been looking forward to seeing them, but I wasn't really 'there' with them.

The texts came thick and fast, and I was trying my best to ignore them whilst we ate lunch that day. I wasn't hungry, but force-fed myself spaghetti-bolognaise, wondering all the time if I could stop my stomach rejecting it. The bitter taste of gastric-acid in my mouth combined with the heavy pasta sauce, searing the back of my throat whilst I pushed it down again.

I plucked up the courage to look at my mobile phone. With tears in my eyes, I reeled through the thirty-or-so text messages that had arrived in the last hour.

The fourth-horseman was 'doing his rounds' and his next blow literally decapitated me:

'Even your children hate you, U CUNT!!! They also think ur a pile of shit just like everyone else!!'

Was this true? Is that what my own children actually thought of me?

I had been 'Gas-lighted' for so long that I didn't know what was true anymore. With tears running down my cheeks, I sheepishly showed my children the text:

'Is that what you think of me, my Darlings?' I quivered.

My children's mouth's opening in disbelief.

'NO Daddy. We LOVE YOU!' they exclaimed.

At that point in time, my children's relationship with Yvette was over forever. My own relationship with Yvette *should* have been over long before that. But the tortured, painful music of the orchestra was still drawing me to the dance floor…

The next day I drove the thirty-five miles down the motorway in my hired van, my heart literally in my mouth. I had my own set of keys to Yvette's house, so I could let myself in and collect what I needed. But would she be home or not? I was mentally torn-in-two, battling with competing thoughts and feelings within myself.

My mind, the 'adult' within me was saying 'Let's hope she's out,' whilst my 'Self', the dominant damaged child within me was praying that she would be in. I arrived and turned the key in the door. There she was; as beautiful as ever. She was calm and collected.

'Do you want some help with the big things?' she helpfully asked. 'I have a bit of time before I go on my date.'

'No, I think I should be fine,' I replied, all the time trying to hold back the flood of tears that I felt could overcome me at any second.

I calmly climbed the stairs to our bedroom, and she followed. I reached into the dresser draw to retrieve my socks, and I couldn't hold it back any longer. I collapsed to the floor, and cried like the small child I was inside; I cried in exactly the way I should have cried when I was beaten by my mother as a child.

'I DON'T WANT TO LEAVE YOU!' I balled.

I was shaking, and I chanted it over and over again, at increasing volume. She put her arms around me and held me, in exactly the same way she had done in that hotel room in Egypt a year earlier. I couldn't do it; I couldn't leave her. She was comforting and soft. She was just the way I wanted her to be all along. She held me, and told me that everything was going to be fine. At last, I thought; at last I have received the love and attention I so desperately craved. I had come 'home'. My personal 'boundaries' were now completely nonexistent. I had succumbed completely, mind, body and soul to the Borderline beast that lay beside me.

The next day, I returned my hired van and accepted my place by her side. There was no resistance left, only love and adulation for her. I was hers, in exactly the way she needed me to be...

Chapter 14

The next few months were a struggle; a tortured struggle within my fractured 'Self'. I felt like a prisoner. I was being held 'captive' by the supplication of food, alcohol and sex. But I was a prisoner of my own making; I was complicit in my capture. It was 'easier' to 'stay put' and deal with the regular abuse, and Yvette's frequent episodes of emotional dysregulation, than it was to leave.

And anyway, I'd tried 'cold turkey' before, so many times, and it hadn't worked. All it had done was cause me more pain in the end.

Throughout this period, my life was filled with mayhem and uncertainly. The dysfunctional merry-go-round of life with Yvette was still at full steam, and I felt like I was getting both dizzy with delight and sick with nausea at the same time. My life was continually punctuated with episodes of 'pushing and pulling'.

Even though Yvette knew that I believed she could have BPD she still 'loved' me, if a Borderline truly does know what 'love' is. However, Instead of seeking therapy, she used my belief about her BPD against me when the next round of devaluation came along; it was but another weapon in her ever-growing arsenal to use against me.

In the same period, I remained in close touch with Liam. He became a good friend. More to the point, he became my *only* friend. I'd lost all my others. He was also a 'survivor' of the abuse that Yvette perpetrated, and I felt like he was a kindred spirit. The problem was I remained a victim, rather than a survivor. But he had done what I fantasised about; leaving Yvette forever. He became my 'hero', in the same way that I was Yvette's hero when her devaluation of me flipped-back to idolisation.

My communication and meetings with Liam became more frequent. I used to see him on the evenings when Yvette was residential on-call at the hospital. I told Yvette that I was seeing an 'old friend' at those times, but it still didn't curtail the torrent of abuse she sent my way when she felt abandoned and alone on those Tuesday evenings.

I learnt from Liam. I wished I was him, because he'd managed to move on from this nightmare I found myself in the midst of.

Liam and Yvette had an ongoing legal battle over access to their children. Liam told me his side of the story, and slowly but surely I learnt to appreciate it. I never did think he was a 'bad' person, like Yvette wanted me to believe he was. I'd held on to my own opinion about Liam throughout all the madness, and I enjoyed being with him.

Children. They had two wonderful children together. Their youngest son was only a new-born when Liam had left Yvette a couple of years previously, and as a father to my own children I appreciated how difficult that must have been for him. Their eldest son was a flourishing little boy, and I loved their children as my own. They were wonderful, precious little souls whom I loved and adored.

But I had witnessed things, things that I had previously ignored and denied. The way that Yvette had raged at Liam on the doorstep, in front of their children; the way that she used to denigrate and devalue Liam in front of their children. And the way that she used to do *everything* she could to ensure her children 'picked' her in preference to Liam. She was 'Gas-lighting' her own children in exactly the same way as she had me. And I knew, deep down, that it was very wrong.

I had previously made so many 'excuses' for her behaviour. 'They're just having a bad divorce,' I convinced myself. 'She's just a bit pissed-off about the way he has treated her,' I excused.

But there was a growing incongruence within me about what was 'real' and what wasn't, and my growing friendship with Liam reinforced that incongruence. If it wasn't for Liam, I would probably still be in that toxic, enmeshed relationship with Yvette. And for that, to him, I literally owe him my life.

I used the limited time I had to myself when Yvette was away on-call to read and learn. When I was immersed in the world of BPD a few months before, I read articles that talked about the 'taker-caretaker' relationship between a Borderline and a co-dependent. But what was co-dependency? Was I really co-dependent? I'd dismissed it as a possibility previously, when I was intent on 'blaming' Yvette's BPD completely for our dysfunction. But could I be? I didn't want to be, because that would mean admitting that there could be something 'wrong' with me, but I had to explore this possibility, to literally save my life.

I gradually 'switched' and moved away from my preoccupation with BPD, to learning about *myself*. Why had I 'chosen' to be in this abusive relationship with Yvette in the first place? Why had I stayed so long, even when I was in danger? Could I truly be 'addicted' to loving her? When I had come across this concept a few months ago, it seemed unthinkable. But could this actually be the case? These were difficult questions, and I was determined to find the answers.

I wanted the answers, because I believed that if I found these answers then I may be able to save two wonderful children, Yvette's children, from growing up as damaged adult-children that both myself and Yvette were. There was a dawning realisation that there was more at stake here than just my 'Self'.

Just like the way the sun peeks out from the horizon at the dawn of a new day and slowly rises in the sky, the dawning of my realisation was gradual; the bright shafts of 'awakening' slowly but surely chased away the 'fog' of my toxic-enmeshment with Yvette. I had to do what I could to save two young children from what I considered a face worse than death; to roam this earth as damaged adult-children.

Was I still 'rescuing' them as co-dependents naturally do? Yes, I recognised that. But their 'souls' were worth saving, even if my own wasn't. The children and my continued relationship with Liam gave me the ability to reinstate my own appreciation of 'reality', rather than remaining in that hall-full of distorted reflections. Yvette was emotionally abusing her own children; and I had to do something about it.

When this realisation dawned, did I believe I still loved Yvette at that time? Yes. Did I still want nothing more than for her to address her behavioural issues so that we could all 'sail happily into the sunset'? Absolutely. Did I want to get 'better' myself, so that I could be better for her and her children? Without a doubt. But my awakening wasn't something I could ignore; it wasn't something I *wanted* to ignore. I chose to listen to 'myself'. And for the first time, probably for

114